Praise for *Do These Sweatpants Make Me Look Single*

This book is everything that Jen is—hilarious, inviting, honest, and deep. There are convicting truths embedded in relatable stories that will bless and benefit anyone who reads this. Jen so graciously and vulnerably welcomes us into her story and offers eternal perspective and hope for whatever season we find ourselves in. Reading this will feel like sitting across from your best friend over a great cup of coffee.

Kallie Terrana
Resident Director, Colorado Christian University

Refreshing, hilarious, raw, and poignant. Jen writes a beautiful story that had me reading late into the night. Whether you are male or female, single or married there is something for you. Grab a pair of sweatpants and coffee and get ready to be inspired to love Jesus just a little more.

Melissa J. MacDonald
Speaker | Author of *Missing* and *Discipline World Changers*

Jen's transformation as a Christian single will keep you hooked until the very last page. Infused with faith-based wisdom, her dating journey is a real-life testimony of what it takes to break free from the patterns that hold us back. This book is a must read for anyone who has ever felt alone and is longing for more.

Elsa Puerner
Young Life Area Director, Denver CO

Witty, intelligent, wise, and introspective. This book is relatable to anyone who has remained single one day beyond the age of 25, but also inspired this married woman with children. The challenges experienced in these pages inspire us all to look deeper for significance. This is not your typical dating book; this is a manual that will capture your attention, make you look long and hard at your life. and inspire you to write a life story that matters.

Heidi Falletta
Pastor | Writer | Adoptive Mom of 3

If you've ever struggled with feeling stuck or left behind in singleness, Jen's heartfelt memoir will help you find the courage to lean in and never give up. It's timely, vulnerable, and super encouraging. Between Jens anecdotes and wit, I found a wealth of wisdom. Get this book!

Chad Bruegman
Pastor | co-founder of Red Rocks Church

As I read the lessons learned between colossal moments of hilarious interactions and tear-filled inner thoughts, I found myself relating through laughter and heartfelt understanding in more ways than one. I, too, have journeyed through seasons challenged with waiting and singleness and love what Jen says: "Singleness is a gift to be explored, not a prison cell to survive." As adventure continually calls my name, I totally agree! My prayer is that Jen will inspire you to show up in courageous and creative ways as a result of reading this book. GRAB A KLEENEX! Prepare to laugh (& cry)! This book is a must-read...single or not.

Wendy J. Henkelman
The Places Between Podcast Host | Author of *Stay in the Story*

A perfect blend of fun and authenticity, this book has plenty of golden nuggets to help you come out on the other side refreshed and renewed in life and love.

Amie Leadingham
Master Certified Relationship Coach

I was hooked from page one, and the book just got better from there! Jen narrates her hilarious (and sometimes heart-breaking) adventures with laugh-out-loud observations and a fresh writing style. Whether you're looking for change, looking for love, or just looking for a fabulous read, this book will leave you smiling and inspired long after you finish the last page.

Karen Bouchard
Author of *Just Hand Over the Chocolate and No One Will Get Hurt*

DO THESE SWEATPANTS MAKE ME LOOK SINGLE?

MY ONE-YEAR QUEST TO LEVEL UP IN HEALTH, FAITH, MONEY & LOVE

JEN CARLSON

ILLUMIFY
MEDIA.COM

Published by
Illumify Media Global
www.IllumifyMedia.com
"Let's bring your book to life!"

Paperback ISBN: 978-1-959099-06-2

Cover design by Adly Elewa

Printed in the United States of America

To Emily,

The one who started it all

Contents

Prologue

"I'm gonna die alone."

~ *Jess,* New Girl

There I was, the total package, every man's dream girl. Past my prime, buried in debt, and fresh off driving probation, I trudged through thick green grass in a yard that was not mine toward a tanned and ringless bachelor who, also, was not mine. Clutched in my left hand was a homemade cheat sheet of one-liners to break the ice.

When it came to striking up conversation with single men, I was not accustomed to failing. Then again, I was not accustomed to trying.

There were many things I excelled at in life, like teaching advanced skin care courses to spas across a multistate region, mentoring teen girls, and squeezing every last drop of Cherry Blossom lip gloss from the tube. So, when my sister Lisa and I decided to launch a dating competition to become better versions of our single selves, I was certain I'd be a natural at that too.

But as the current scoreboard reflected, I trailed my sister by a landslide. And when it came to living my best life, I still had a long way to go.

Sidestepping bags of Miracle-Gro, I took a step toward the bachelor, otherwise known as McHottie. He and I had been in a complicated, long-distance relationship for over three years, with most of our complications stemming from the fact that he didn't know I existed, and our long-distance status being the bird's-eye view my kitchen window had of his townhouse, three doors to the north.

We had greeted one another with cordial smiles and nods on my occasional morning walks, but I swore this time was going to be different. This time I was going to walk straight up to him and say the carefully crafted line my lips had been reciting the entire month.

If I did, 10 points would be mine. And if I could work up the courage to give him a way to contact me if he was interested, I'd score an extra 50 points too.

Still unnoticed, I took another step, careful to avoid the power tools that littered his front lawn. McHottie picked up a two-by-four, slicing it in two. His Bluetooth speaker pumped the bass while my heart matched the beat. Just then, my movement caught his dark smoky eyes. Powering down his table saw, he stood in a cloud of sawdust, like a wall of pure testosterone.

I gulped, and loudly. All woodland creatures scattered.

My tongue started to swell; a sweat mustache began to form. I was now just inches from his project, inches from his body. What was my line again? Thoughts buzzed; my mouth went dry.

As the sun hit his glistening brow, my brain could only register one thing: *Hey there, handsome. Do my lips taste like bacon, or is it just me?* Before the words left my mouth, my internal self-talk roared to life: *Abort! That is not your line. Repeat: that is definitely not your line.*

"Can I help you?" he said, brushing strands of adorable brown curls away from his brow. I tried to assert a well-executed flirtatious eye flutter, but appeared to have something in my eye instead. Taking a deep breath, I raced to recover my words.

Whose idea was this dating competition anyway?

Yet I knew there were two answers to that question. First, our six-month challenge was about so much more than dating. And also, the crazy brainchild was mine.

Chapter 1 | Stuck

"I yearn for more from my life. I yearn for purpose."

~ Wonder Woman

Before I tell you how the story with neighbor McHottie ends, it's important that you know why I, an introverted, single woman in her midthirties, buried in debt and straight off driving probation, was earning points for trolling through my neighbor's lawn.

Because this book is about my quest to get unstuck and create the life I'd always dreamed of, it's best if we start at the beginning—back to a time when the only major complication I faced was which Netflix series I should watch next.

Late one August night, seven months prior, my cell phone rang. On the surface it was just your average phone call, nothing flashy or earth-shattering about it. Instead, it arrived like a gentle breeze, sweeping in at just the right time, tipping over one little domino deep inside me.

Little did I know as I picked up the phone, revival was about to begin. And my life would never be the same.

The Phone Call

The hands on the clock read 10:14 p.m., and the remote control was under my complete power. My lips tasted like brownie batter with a hint of marshmallow fluff, and so did my chin, for that matter.

Staring at me in silence was my date, frozen and expressionless. "You are amazing," I whispered. There was no response. Creamy containers of Ben & Jerry's were good for a lot of things, but conversation apparently was not one of them.

Tension slung between Elizabeth Bennet and Mr. Darcy on my TV as I snuggled into my worn gray couch cushions, reciting every line. They stood in the middle of a rainstorm, soaked to the bone, prideful and prejudiced, still unaware of their undying love for the other. I jumped at the loud clap of onscreen thunder, swept away by a story that was four million times better than my own.

It was Friday night, and I was introverting. Hard.

STATS: 33 years old. Regional spa trainer. 5'10". Single.

Double-dipping back into my pint, I contemplated my chances of winning gold if freestyle ice-cream eating ever became an Olympic event. "High" to "Very High" seemed like an appropriate estimate of my talents, I decided.

Just then, my cell phone rang. It was my youngest sister, Emily.

STATS: 23 years old. College senior. 5'6". Single.

"Wait right there," I instructed my British friends, hitting pause on the remote.

"Hey, Em!" We were the bookend sisters. I was the oldest of the four kids, and she was the youngest. An entire decade spanned between us, and she held a tender place in my heart because of it.

Emily was a psychology major at a small private Christian college in Indiana. She was always spilling over with deep thoughts, which is what I love about her. We were both introspective and deep feelers, with just the right amount of sass.

Beyond that, Emily was everything I wasn't in one hot little package. Mozart on the piano, Pelé on the field. Collagen levels in their prime. Adele on the mic, Pocahontas in the wild. Teeth as straight as an arrow and white as a baby snow owl. Just enough freckles to be so adorable you want to stare at her all day, but you've got errands to run, so it's not going to happen. She was not only the youngest but also the hottest and most talented of all four of us kids. I adore her.

Being halfway across the country, she occasionally called me for advice. We'd always end our convos by joking she could pay me in future face-lifts when I was old and haggard and she was still young and full of life and face volume. But that night was going to be different. Her words would change me.

"I've been telling my friends at college about you, Jen . . ." Her voice trailed off.

Beaming, I straightened. "Oh really?" My chocolate mustache curled into a smile.

"The other night we were talking about how hard it is to be single when everybody is dating and getting engaged. Some girls were wondering what was wrong with them, or shared how they just want to be married, or the fact that we're just getting so . . . so . . . old."

(Me: chokes on my Ben & Jerry's.)

"But I told them," she continued, her confidence strong and high, "'You guys, it's okay. Both my sisters are older, and they're both still single. And they just live life to the fullest. They live these amazing, purpose-driven lives.'"

Her voice was steady, certain, sure. Confident that Lisa and I were living the unshakable dream, totally killing it in the world of singleness. To her college friends, we were now a symbol of hope, a beacon of light. True poster models for nonstop, adventurous single living.

Glancing down at my waistline, I noted my sweatpants had crept dangerously high, slightly twisted, causing a major wedgie. My left sock hung halfway off my foot; the right had a hole near the second toe.

My eyes traveled upward, pausing on the words stretched across my heather-gray hoodie: "It Took Me 30 Years to Look This Good." Chocolate dripped through the letter *G*, and it was in that moment that it hit me. If I was the new poster model for young single babes, then forever hopeless they would all surely remain.

Have I Missed My Chance?

I remembered the age of twenty-three so clearly, I could feel the tightening in my chest. Spring filled the Minnesota air. I was drenched in mermaid-blue chiffon, walking down the plush burgundy carpeted aisle as a bridesmaid in my century-old childhood church. Wedding season had officially begun.

My long dark hair was piled into tight curls on top of my head, shiny and a little crisp, thanks to half a can of Big Sexy hair spray. A slightly smudged DIY manicure in Fee-Fi-Fo Plum clasped a bouquet of pale pastels at my waist in front of me.

According to the white goggle marks around my eyes, I was an ambitious shade of tan for my Scandinavian heritage, compliments of the "Unlimited UV + Me" package at Totally Tan & Spa. Rumor had it, ultraviolet rays cleared breakouts, so I smiled and nodded, and did what the nice rumors told me to do.

This was, of course, before I went to beauty school to become an aesthetician. Before I learned you shouldn't trust every trending solution out there. Even the ones I'd grown up believing about how to find love.

Lifting my hem, I stepped past the twenty-four-year-old groom and stood on the stairs under the choir loft. Then the music shifted, the double doors reopened, and the congregation stood. My heart warmed as one of my dearest childhood friends stepped across the threshold and took my breath away.

That was the beginning of the Year of Fifteen Weddings. Those double doors continued to open as one dear friend or cousin after another walked down the aisle.

Growing up, no one ever said out loud that there was a nine-step plan to becoming a twenty-something Christian woman success. Then again, no one had to. There was a rhythm to what I observed, an unspoken gold standard. A sweet and simple recipe for girls like me: ones who loved the Lord, loved others, and followed the rules.

College first. Meet a godly young man. Guy pursues girl. Graduate. Marry young. Land a career. Buy a home. Raise a family. Live happily ever after. In that order.

And that nine-step plan did happen—for dozens of my sweet cousins. For my fellow volunteer teammates in Young Life. It happened for both my roommates, along with all my dearest childhood friends. Yet despite my wishing, my hoping, my praying, it did not happen for me.

Truth be told, I was a bit of a renegade after high school. Instead of going to a private Christian college like my close friends, I went to the local community college, or "PBU" as some of us joked. It stood for Pole Barn University, which was not its real name but felt more accurate since most of my classes were in a winterized metal shed that was sold at the local Fleet Farm.

It was during my dreamy stint at PBU that I took philosophy twice, met exactly zero datable guys, and fell head over heels in love with Young Life, a Christian nonprofit I volunteered for.

Instead of plowing through college, I went the leisurely route. Transferring to a junior college closer to Minneapolis, I dropped to part-time, moved into an apartment with two newly engaged friends, and took a job on Young Life staff working with teens.

Needless to say, I missed the memo they passed out at the private Christian colleges: "Ring by spring, or your money back!" All right, so the schools didn't *actually* hand out that memo. But it was indeed the joke that floated around many campuses. The joke that always seemed to come true.

The Year of Fifteen Weddings

During the Year of Fifteen Weddings, I dove waist deep into taffeta, charmeuse, and chiffon in every color but white. I bought bridesmaids dresses in bulk, giftwrapped slinky lingerie, frosted mini cupcakes, and ordered cans of hair spray by the case.

Thanks to Target, Williams Sonoma, and Bed Bath & Beyond, I watched my besties sail straight from dorm life to the proud owners of well-equipped kitchens and Pinterest-perfect homes.

Overnight, their bath towel collections became fluffier than any of us ever dreamed possible. Shiny, freestanding KitchenAid mixers were poised stoically on kitchen counters across the Twin Cities metro. Old underwear was upgraded to rainbows of lace and silk.

By the following June came the grand finale. Both of my roommates got married two weeks apart. One by one, boxes were carried out our apartment door by fiancés and proud dads.

I'll never forget the final wedding of that year, coming home to our dark apartment alone. Heels in one hand, wilted bouquet in the other. My twin bed and small dresser looked like doll furniture in that large two-bedroom flat.

Pinholes and scuff marks were scattered across blank white walls where pictures and posters and life and memories had once been on display. And as I walked to the bathroom to brush my teeth and unpin my curls, my footsteps echoed down the hall.

It was the end of an era. Like the last episode in a series finale, all the characters were moving on. *College first. Meet a godly young man. Guy pursues girl. Graduate. Marry young . . .*

I couldn't bear to say it out loud, but that year flattened me. I was twenty-four years old and felt too young to feel so behind, to feel so alone.

Two months later, I took an internship at a Young Life camp in Oregon. Everything I owned fit into the back of my small station wagon as I made the twenty-eight-hour cross-country drive west. Upon arrival I was given a bedroom in a duplex packed with twelve singles, all in our twenties. Seven on the girls' side, five on the guys'.

We all signed an agreement not to date one another for the entire year, a rule put into place after past intern love triangles. In the snap of a finger, I no longer felt left behind, or that my life was offtrack. The pure joy of having other single friends hit me like an electric shock, knocking a strong beat back into my heart.

For one year, our crew of guys and girls moved in a pack. We skied Mount Bachelor, snowshoed the Cascades, and piled into trucks, bumping down dirt roads to float the John Day River.

We worked together, prayed together, served kids together. Then each evening in our backyard we bellied up to a long wooden table one of the guys built. Dinners lasted hours, rich in conversation after long, hearty twelve-hour days of work.

When the internship ended the following October, we all divided back across the country where we came from. I moved to Minneapolis; forty-eight hours later, I started beauty school. Two weeks after that, I walked down that same plush burgundy carpet at my hometown church, a bridesmaid in another friend's wedding.

I wasn't prepared for the devastating loneliness that would overcome me after that internship. As it turned out, life had kept moving while I was away. Engagements and weddings were now old news. In their place came job promotions, upgrades to bigger homes, couples' vacations to Cabo. Then Christmas card season came, the flannel-clad reminders of the things I hoped for yet still did not have.

At the end of that winter, right after graduating beauty school and celebrating my twenty-sixth birthday, my brother Brian married his fiancé, Ashley. He was twenty-four and a recent finance grad; she was twenty-one and graduating early as a youth pastor. And I had a hot-off-the-press license to body wax as I walked that same childhood church aisle as a bridesmaid once again.

Being part of each celebration always brought me incredible joy. Every wedding was perfection, unique in its own colors, flowers, and style. Yet there was always one thing that stayed the same. *Me.* Standing in the crowd, brow still damp from dancing the night away, I'd cheer as each newlywed couple ran to their getaway car.

Waving my sparkler until all that was left was a curl of smoke, like a birthday candle after your biggest wish, I'd watch their taillights fade into the distance. And then I would climb into my car and drive home—alone.

Will that ever be me? my heart would ask, though never out loud. *Have I missed my chance?* But I found that it hurt too much to wonder, and it hurt too much to want. So, I put those very real desires of my heart in a box – the desire for love and for companionship. I closed the lid and pushed them out of sight and out of mind.

As I wandered through my late twenties, I made a conscious decision that I wasn't going to be one of "those girls." You know the type: pitied, sad, wallowing, desperate for love, waiting for a man to complete her. I wasn't going to waste my life chasing love.

The plan, I determined, was that dating would happen naturally, then successfully, all when the time was right. That was the rumor anyway. The invisible nine-step plan I had come to believe in. As a faith-centered woman, it was my naïve understanding that trust, prayer, and time were the only ingredients required to find love.

And so, I trusted.

And I prayed.

And I waited.

I developed my career, landing a job as a traveling trainer for a medspa company, training nurses and aestheticians how to use exciting machines, like cellulite-reducing vacuums, hair-follicle–blasting lasers, and wellness pods shaped like mini spaceships. There weren't many men around, but it was an interesting gig nonetheless. You'd be surprised how fun it is to vacuum booties and thighs.

At age twenty-eight I enrolled in night school for my bachelor's degree in communications at Northwestern, a lovely private Christian college in St. Paul. On my drive onto campus each night, my headlights would beam onto a giant boulder that newly engaged day students would spray paint their initials on.

I imagined every young college sophomore girl walking past that big rock, dreaming of the day she'd be the one to paint her name next to a guy's, inside a big red heart. Then I'd keep driving. Between working fifty hours a week and going to class each night, I was far too busy to date. I only had time to dream.

By the time I slipped on that cap and gown, I was twenty-nine years old, an old maid among the graduating day students, and an older maid compared to all my dearest friends whose adorable pregnant bellies bumped along together. Some with their first, others on their second, a few with their third.

To sum things up, I didn't date much in my twenties, and when I finally joined eHarmony toward the end of that decade, it was because I felt very much alone as I walked long hospital hallways, pink or blue balloons in hand.

There was a longing inside me to start something new. I began applying for jobs out West, and a few months later, I got the fresh start I was praying for.

Fresh Starts

Three months shy of turning thirty, I started a job as a regional spa trainer for a beauty brand in Denver. Out West, I discovered, not everyone marries right after college. I joined a coed singles life group at my new church. I gave online dating a real chance, went on a lot of dates. I even had a short-lived relationship.

But as many singles can attest to, the heart needs to take the occasional breather from online dating. So, I took a break.

Then work travel picked up. The coed singles group disbanded, and I started a women's group instead. Weekends were reserved for girlfriends and catching up on exciting things like 401K paperwork, laundry, REM cycles, and expense reports. Then a new Netflix show started. Then another, and another . . .

And suddenly it was nearly four years later, and I was in my midthirties watching *Pride and Prejudice* alone on a Friday night, sitting on a pile of student loan bills, adding an extra loop to my belt every few years, being nominated by my gorgeous college sister for the "Living Your Best Self" award.

The truth was, no matter how tightly I had sealed that lid in my heart, the desire for love and companionship remained. And in the quietest hours when Netflix was turned off and my apartment went quiet, I would take that box out and look at my hopes, now intertwined with excuses. I would pray that God would see me, that he would not forget me, and that he'd send a rescue boat my way.

Preferably a dreamboat, I'd add. *The tall, dark, and handsome variety.*

And so, it was on that Friday night, with a sticky spoon in my left hand and phone pressed to my ear with my right, that I felt my views on love, on dating, on singleness tug inside me, begging to be challenged. I didn't know what it meant. But something told me it was time to do a little unboxing.

"Thanks for listening, Jen. Like always, put it on my tab."

"No, Em. Thank you. This one's on me. I love you."

"Love you too."

Hanging up the phone, I stared for a moment into the abyss called my thirty-something life. Then I took a deep breath and called our other sister, Lisa.

Hashtag Cool Girl

"Hey, Jen," Lisa picked up, groggy, as if half-asleep.

STATS: 29 years old. Young Life area director. 5'3". Single.

"Hey, Lis," I responded. "What are you up to?" I heard crunching in the background.

"Lying on the couch playing Candy Crush and eating a sleeve of Girl Scout cookies." She paused. "Why? What are you doing?"

"Lying on the couch watching *Pride and Prejudice*, eating a pint of Ben & Jerry's." The line fell silent. "Wanna Zoom?"

"Sure. See you in five."

Minutes later, I was seated in front of the computer, staring at Lisa and trying to ignore the matching four o' clock shadows between both our brows.

Her living room was dark, with the exception of her face, which was propped up by a couch cushion and lit up like a jack-o'-lantern from the glow of the screen. There was a twinkle in her root-beer-brown eyes, something they always did, for reasons no one ever knew but her.

Lisa was the third sibling, our lighthearted middle sister. She was a few years younger than me and Brian, and over six years older than Emily. She had my deep, hearty laugh, which we likened to those old cantankerous, heckling Muppet brothers who cracked themselves up.

We also shared the same long brown hair, though I colored my premature grays the first week of every month while she wore hers au naturel. She had Emily's warm, summery skin, sprinkled with the same spunky freckles and her same artistic flair.

In other ways, Lisa marched to the beat of her own drum. She loved quirky thrift store finds and owned a small black-and-white dwarf bunny. His name was Captain Jack Jack Oswald the Lucky Rabbit, which she claimed her Young Life kids came up with. Though it sounded like something she'd come up with too.

Lisa is easy to please, loves a crowd, never a care in the world. Rational, steady, low maintenance. A mascara-and-Chapstick kind of girl. She's the shortest sister by a landslide, more than half a foot shorter than me.

Staring at our images, I noted we each had one more chin than I'd like to own up to.

"Just got off the phone with Emily," I announced.

"Oh yeah?"

"Yeah." My voice was flat. I had a lot on my mind.

Over the next several minutes, I unpacked the conversation I had with our youngest sister. It was hard to argue the irony of her flawlessly timed Friday-night call. The hard truth was these types of weekends were becoming more of the norm than Lisa and I cared to admit.

"Okay, how about this," I said. "Let's tally the number of dates we have each been on in the last six months; then we'll add them together."

The results? Her dates + my dates = 1 date.

I'm not a math whiz by any means, but even I knew that one date in six months between two single women who were very interested in not being single was not good odds. It was numbers like those that kept girls like us in the snack aisle for far too long.

As I looked at our results, visions of a little friendly competition began to form. As a major goal setter with a flair for creative and borderline-crazy ideas, I stared at Lisa. There was a glint of mischief in my eyes.

"What if we started a dating competition?"

Lisa raised a brow. "Is that a dare?"

"Absolutely," I said, scrambling for a pen.

I still have the screenshot I snapped of us that Friday night. Drunk on sugar and bad ideas, we are smiling like fools, sporting near identical sloppy side ponytails and activewear that had yet to be active.

There was excitement in the air with a side of guilt. One, because we were devising a dating competition, and two, because we were holding up half-eaten late-night snacks. As for which caused the excitement and which caused the side of guilt, your guess is as good as mine.

"All right, let's get this party started," I said, flipping to a fresh, clean page in a brand-new hot pink notebook. Because: nothing screams "hashtag cool girl" and "Friday night rager" like a bottle of Tums and stack of school supplies.

The Plan

The basic premise of our dating challenge came together in a flash. Thank you, high-fructose corn syrup. Without you, our delirium never would have become a reality.

The plan? We would design a six-month competition, a series of social experiments, each month with its own theme. Every set of challenges would help us a) increase confidence, b) find freedom, and c) enhance ourselves as single women. (Nonsurgically, of course.)

There would be points.

There would be prizes.

But only one of us would be crowned the Dating Champion of the World. (Cue dramatic drums beating in a distant land.)

"Are you sure you're up to the challenge, Lis?" I teased. "You should know, when it comes to fake crowns and fictitious titles, I stop at nothing."

"Uh, Jen," she responded, popping a Thin Mint into her mouth. "You've got ice cream dripping down your hoodie." Midchomp, she added, "And your chin."

Ownership

As the inevitable sugar crash set in, we made a pact to do things differently, at least just for six months. Emily's phone call had come like a lifeboat to our complacency, inviting us to ask ourselves, *Am I really living the unshakable dream of being a confident, thriving single woman?* Something felt missing.

As much as we wanted to believe it was an Instagrammable #plusone we lacked, we had a feeling that once we started to do a little unboxing, we might find something more.

As I grabbed the mouse to log off for the night, I noticed my car's license plate tabs and registration sitting on top of a pile of student loan bills. The tabs expired in July. It was now the middle of August.

"Dang it," I said, shaking my head.

"Everything okay?"

"Yeah, I just keep forgetting to put the new tabs on my car," I responded. "No big deal, I'll do it tomorrow."

I looked down at my hot pink notebook, now filled with notes and ideas to revamp our single lives. Change was in the air; I could feel it.

After air-hugging Lisa, I shut down my computer and threw away my empty pint, then went to bed. All night I dreamed of a new life. A better life.

By the next day, I had forgotten all about the expired tabs.

Chapter 2 | Goji Berry Red

Han Solo: How are we doing?
Luke Skywalker: The same as always.
Han Solo: That bad, huh?

~ Star Wars, Return of the Jedi

Lights flashed in my rearview mirror as I sat red-faced behind the wheel of my rusted 2006 Ford Focus on the side of the road, four blocks from home. Outside my window, the officer's thick hand flipped to a second page as he scribbled his report. White-knuckling the wheel, I imagined what he wrote:

Female driver, midthirties, applied new Goji Berry
red lipstick at stoplight en route to Target. Impressed by
its vibrant hue in rearview mirror, her foot slipped off the
brake, rolling her car into the stopped vehicle in front of
her. Speed: 9 mph.

Damage to other vehicle: none.

Damage to perpetrator's vehicle: broken head-
light, smashed fender, and Goji Berry lipstick, absolutely
everywhere.

My daydream was interrupted by a knock on the window. Rolling it down, I attempted a weak smile. There was no use in going for the flirtatious eye flutter; those skills were worse than my driving record.

"Ma'am." The officer leaned down, slipping a white piece of paper into my car. "I'm issuing you an eight-point violation for the crash and for driving under the influence."

"Under the influence, Officer?" My eyes widened.

"Of lipstick," he said solemnly.

I wanted to argue, but the clown-like red ring smeared around my lips, all over the steering wheel, and across my forehead was all the evidence he needed.

He passed me a second white slip, adding, "And here's a four-point violation for the expired tabs." Straightening, he nodded. "Be careful out there." Then he turned toward his squad car and walked away.

I stared at the triple-digit dollar amounts stamped on my tickets, then glanced at my banged-up hood, mentally calculating the deductible and insurance increase. My head dropped back against the headrest, and I closed my eyes, letting the weight of my financial situation sink in. It was no secret money was tight. This was the last thing I needed.

Turning on my blinker, I puttered onto the highway. Cars in the left lane zipped past me, one right after another. I swear each of them was newer than the last—hot, young, happy couples behind every wheel, their tanned skin and five-karat diamonds glittering against the Colorado sun.

I chugged along, picking up speed. My hood rattled against the wind.

"Can't a girl just catch a break?" I groaned at the sky as if God himself was the one who needed to be paying more attention.

No sooner had the words left my mouth when a strong gust of wind whipped across the highway, snapping loose the front latch of my hood. I watched in horror as it sailed back at me, smashing against my windshield, glass shattering, tires swerving like Cruella de Vil high on dalmatians.

Instantly I lost all highway visibility. As I barreled down the freeway, the hood of my car stood vertically in the air, *Tommy Boy* style, creating a total blackout. Car horns blared from every direction and I braced for impact as my body flung left, then right.

Scream praying was all I could do.

"LETTTT MEEEE LIVVVVE!"

Just then, my tires hit gravel. Slamming on the brakes, I slid to a stop, dust swirling around me. My hood dropped down and clicked back into place as if nothing ever happened.

Glancing in the rearview mirror, I was startled to see skin as white as a ghost, rings of black mascara, and a wild stain of goji.

Heart pounding, adrenaline racing, I closed my eyes, dropping my clown face to the steering wheel. That's when I heard it. In the distance came an all-too-familiar sound.

"No, no, no," I groaned.

Sirens.

Driving Probation

Within two weeks, I was summoned to the Denver Police Department, where an unpleasant, portly fellow assigned to desk duty impatiently tapped his foot as I relinquished my Colorado driver's license.

I guess I couldn't blame him for his sour scowl. He had to deal with daydreaming drivers like me all day, begging him for mercy, bribing him with donuts.

As luck would have it, there is a limit to the number of driving violations that can be acquired in a six-month time period. And my Goji Berry lips? Guilty as charged.

Clipping my license in two, he barked, "You've got a red license for the next six months." He continued with my restrictions. During probation, I could drive only to work and to one preassigned grocery store listed on my paperwork.

It took some begging, and I am under oath as to the number of donuts that sealed the deal, but by the time I left his office, one preapproved church and one preapproved gym were typed on my list as well.

As for my desperate pleas to add the top forty Denver first-date hot spots? Denied. If I was caught driving anywhere else, he threatened, my license would be gone for good.

Dragging my feet out his office door, through the hallway, and down the sidewalk to the parking lot, I stopped in front of my car. The crumpled fender was a near perfect match to the state of my heart.

Off in the distance an early snow had capped the upper Rockies; a chill in the air revealed winter was not far behind it. In a few months, Christmas card photos would start rolling in—yet another reminder of all the things I did not have: love, the deed to a house, a growing brood of kids, the ability to drive to a date without getting arrested, peace on earth.

Pulling out my phone, I scrolled to Lisa's number, then took a deep breath and hit dial. Our dating challenge had been scheduled to start that month; our lives had been scheduled to change. *Not anymore.* I sighed, staring at my duct-taped fender.

"Hey, Jen," she answered.

"Hey, sister." My voice dragged on the words as I tightened my grip around my provisional license. "I've got some good news and I've got some bad news."

"Okay."

"So, the bad news is . . ." I hesitated. "There is no good news."

Church. Work. Gym.

Lying on the couch, I cracked open the fortune cookie from my Chinese takeout, desperate for some life direction. It was Saturday afternoon. Two full weeks had passed of being imprisoned inside the four walls of my apartment, where I had managed to log record-breaking numbers of *The Office* reruns and Uber Eats deliveries.

As it turned out, I was left disappointed, both by my fortune ("You are the crispy noodle in the vegetarian salad of life.") and by my luck (in that I had none).

The hot pink dating challenge notebook stared at me from my large refurbished oak coffee table. Inside its first few pages were all the preliminary ideas for our competition. Quirky social experiments to help us meet men. Comical one-liners to try on guys. Lists of places menfolk seemed to hang out.

But a tube of lipstick had changed all that. Lisa responded as she always does in crisis: offering a casual shrug and a mildly reassuring "We'll figure it out." And I reacted as I do in such terrible times: twenty-seven pages of journal entries, hours of verbal processing, chocolate therapy, countless hours staring at the wall while buried under piles of down blankets, crushing internal guilt trips.

A week after my sentencing, I'd received more bad news; I was denied a work advancement I had been giving my heart and soul to achieve. It was the second year in a row I was rejected for the opportunity, and it crushed me.

Without that promotion, I was barely squeaking by. Denver was in the top most expensive US cities to live in, and I was making less than the average household income. My rent was increasing that month, and my car had less than a breath left in it.

I also had over $23,000 in student debt I was hacking away at. My starting balance had been nearly $50,000, and although I was proud of my progress, I was tired of digging out of that hole. For over four years I had been paying double payments each month. The only solution to digging out faster, it seemed, was to get promoted. But we all know how that story ended.

Rubbing my face, I sighed. The fatigue was killing me, and I knew deep down it wasn't just about money. While I loved my job, it was hard to stay healthy traveling across a multistate region. Eating out for every meal was the norm.

But if I was being honest, my eating habits weren't that different at home. My knees ached, and I was out of shape, lacking motivation, and too tired to change it.

Reaching over the hot pink notebook, I grabbed some half-empty takeout. Netflix had gone black, the screen frozen with one question: "Are you still watching *The Office*?"

I wanted to hit play. Life didn't feel so hard when I didn't have to think about it. I could delay it, at will, whenever it felt a little too much. But deep down I knew waiting around for my life to begin was no life at all.

Setting down the carton, I picked up the pink notebook. A single piece of paper stuck out. It had an impressive government seal at the top: "State of Colorado — Department of Motor Vehicles." It was my probation paperwork.

As I scanned the document, my eyes stopped midpage. There, in three simple twelve-point words, was my sentencing:

CHURCH. WORK. GYM.

In that moment, I didn't have to journal or pray or wonder or meditate on what my next move should be. I just knew.

Maybe I can't change everything about my life, I thought. *But I can change something.*

Make Room

"It's been a long time, my friends," I whispered, staring at the cardio machines lined up like rows of soldiers at attention in my gym. Each one had a great view of the wall-to-wall TVs that were playing an assortment of trashy music videos, college football games, and soap opera reruns.

Except one.

Halfway down the row was an elliptical situated directly in front of a floor-to-ceiling second-story window. Sunbeams filtered through the glass, hitting the machine at just the right angle. It was as if heaven itself were calling me to it.

Climbing on, I began to move. A petite Lycra-clad beauty jammed to my left; another size 2 bounced to my right. My legs felt stiff, and thick as tree trunks, lifting, then pushing, then lifting again. I watched my reflection towering between theirs; slow and awkward, like a three-legged, snaggle-tooth Chihuahua shoved into the ring at "best in show."

Beyond the glass in front of me stood a tall, half-barren tree. Cool September winds had done their job, pulling and plucking branches clean. Just a handful of crisp leaves hung on for dear life, rattling in the breeze. It was being stripped of everything and left with nothing.

The tree faded as my reflection came back into view.

And that's when I heard them. Two words. Not audibly, but loudly just the same. Deep inside my soul they pounded like a drumbeat: *Make room.*

Before I could question their meaning, a strong gust of wind hit the tree, whisking a swirl of leaves into the air. The steady whisper came again.

Make room.

#LivingMyBestCriminalLife

That September, I took responsibility for the fact that my life was lacking in three major areas beyond just dating:

1. I was financially stuck.
2. My lifestyle was not healthy.
3. And I'd been swimming in the shallow end when it came to my faith.

With one clip of my driver's license, my life had gone from busy to simple. Jam-packed to a bit lonely. But there was a holiness to the loneliness, whispers in the quiet. And I did not want to waste the strange gift given to me.

That month, I wrote three commitments in my journal. The first was that no matter what I would be debt free by the middle of the following September, exactly one year. Crunching the numbers, it was mathematically impossible on my salary with increasing rent and Denver's high cost of living. No matter how much I chopped and slashed my budget, there was just no possible way.

I wrote it down anyway.

Next, I planned to lose two to four pounds per month for the next year. It was a weight range I'd been in before—still plus-size but healthy. I wanted to accomplish this without following any special diet or giving up any food groups. Elimination and dieting worked for some people, but I'd learned that mind-set was not for me. I wanted a balanced approach with an "all foods fit" mentality.

Lastly, I wanted to read the Bible front to back, something I'd never done, even if it took a year or more. It was no coincidence that the day after my date with the elliptical machine, the daily reading in my devotional book was titled "Make Room for God." If there's one thing I knew, it's that if I truly wanted change in my life, it needed to start by spending more time with him.

I had made goals in the past—lots of them. In fact, I considered myself a goal nerd, one of those vision-board buffs and checklist-obsessed firstborns. Yet more often than not, I'd lose motivation before crossing the finish lines.

Historically, I piled big, hairy audacious goals onto an already bursting plate. Perhaps that's why habits rarely stuck. So I vowed to try a new approach during probation. Instead of adding more stuff in, I would focus on a life of less—and in a sense making room for what mattered most.

Lisa and I rescheduled our challenge to start after probation—that is, if we were both still single. The new start date? April 1—aka Fool's Day. Because when else would two single women kick off a dating competition?

Relentless and Steady Subtraction

That September, I canceled Netflix, sold my TV on Craigslist, and downgraded my cell plan to a regional carrier with a data plan fit for grandmothers. Immediately, I turned around and threw that chunk of change on my smallest loan, like a young Karate white belt annihilating their first board.

My calendar had already been wiped clean thanks to probation. I had nothing but time, and I got crazy intentional with how I spent it.

First stop: social media. Temporarily deactivating my accounts helped me become laser focused on my goals.

On Tuesday nights, I started volunteering with Financial Peace University at my church. I'd taken the class before, and it was motivating to be surrounded by other FPU nuts. I loved cheering when someone would cut up their credit cards in front of the group. And I always got teary eyed when callers on the national radio show did their "Debt-Free Scream."

My brother, Brian, and his wife, Ashley, were also doing the program in Minnesota, climbing out of their student loan debt. I asked him to be my accountability partner, and we started texting about our wins every few weeks. Knowing we'd be checking in kept me on the straight and narrow.

Thursday evenings I signed up to host a church life group for women in their thirties. There were seven of us—a mix of single and married, mothers and not. We ate brownies, competed in juvenile icebreakers, and worked through Jennie Allen's Bible study *Restless: Because You Were Made for More*. Exactly all-of-it was what my soul needed to keep me going during probation.

In October I started meal planning. Instead of ordering in or opening my fridge and praying dinner would magically appear, on Sundays I grocery shopped after church, then cranked up the music, prepping fun new dinners all afternoon.

Balsamic pork chops, Hasselback sweet potatoes, fresh green beans drizzled with sun-dried tomato butter.

Southwestern avocado turkey burgers, tangy herb yogurt sauce, spiced potato wedges.

Grilled Caesar chicken sandwich paired with roasted carrot fries.

Coincidence or not, that's the month my pants began to feel looser. I was still going to the gym a few nights each week after work. But it was those balanced meals replacing a heavy takeout diet that really started to make me feel great.

In November a group of close friends pooled their money to rent a ski condo in Breckenridge for the winter. They invited me to join, but it wasn't in my budget. It was the same answer I'd given for happy hours, a snowmobiling adventure, and a group going to a holiday play.

Three months into probation, I stopped hearing from a lot of people. Blame the short days, cold nights, or the fact I was stuck in the burbs with less than a few nickels to my name and even fewer driving privileges. My life group took a break for the holidays; FPU wrapped up too.

Winter's solitude was heavy, and my heart ached as I hung ornaments on the tree alone. Piles of big happy red and green cards arrived, filled with good friends snuggled in matching candy cane pj's with spouses and kids. Meanwhile, my dinner table was set for one.

To combat the isolation, I picked up a second job working evenings and weekends at a mall department store in children's clothing.

Each shift, I prayed no one from my corporate life would spot me wearing that vest and elf ears while folding piles of newborn clothing some crazed Black Friday shopper had dumped behind the limited-edition KitchenAid mixer display.

To layer insult to injury, I was trudging through Leviticus and Numbers in my Bible reading plan. No offense, Jesus. It was just a lot of temple measurements to take in after a sixteen-hour workday.

But each day, through the humdrum and in the quiet, I continued to hear that still, small voice: *Make room.* And so, I did.

By the time the calendar flipped to February, a funny thing happened. My stress was lower; my priorities were shifting. I was performing better at work. Overwhelming piles of paperwork were becoming obsolete; cluttered inboxes a thing of the past.

I was thick into the most mundane six months of my entire life. Bedtime medicine rounds at the nursing home had more thrills. But *making room* was doing something to me.

Or perhaps it was doing something for me.

Change Is in the Air

"You've lost weight," Lisa observed as our arms pumped in tandem on side-by-side elliptical machines at my gym. It was mid-February, and she was in Colorado for annual Young Life meetings. Also, she was right.

My clothes fit better than they had in years; not to mention, my energy levels had skyrocketed to those of a twenty-seven-year-old, which I know impresses you. We were squeezing in a quick workout, then heading to brunch to celebrate my birthday, followed by a scenic drive to Red Rocks Amphitheatre before her flight that night.

"Yeah, I've lost a few pounds," I said, straightening my shoulders. "Thanks for noticing."

Turning back to the floor-to-ceiling second-story window in front of us, I watched the ice-tipped tree branches sway and stretch across the cold gray sky. It was the same view I'd studied three to five times each week for nearly six months, the same tree I watched lose its crisp autumn leaves before settling in for a cold lifeless winter.

There was something comforting about that tall stoic tree. I couldn't put my finger on it. In a strange way, it seemed to understand what I was going through, what it was like to slog through a long humdrum season alone.

With that tree as our witness, Lisa and I began resurrecting plans for our competition. That winter, we had each read *How to Get a Date Worth Keeping* by Christian psychologist Dr. Henry Cloud. His book is packed with practical coaching tips along with inspiration when it came to our own challenges.

But most of all, we loved how Cloud describes the purpose of dating. Instead of focusing on finding the right person, he encourages singles to focus on becoming better versions of themselves.

That morning, we explored questions like *How would you describe your best self?* and *At the end of six months, who do you want to be?* It didn't take long for my responses to blend with hers, and hers to blend with mine.

My best self?

> She is courageous, self-confident, financially free.
> She is growing in her relationship with God.
> Healthy, adventurous, a woman of her word.
> She is living with purpose, experiencing the community, not getting stuck in the same old routines.
> She doesn't wait for an invitation, but gets out there, creates opportunities.
> She is prepared and brave.
> Intentional.
> Playful.
> Wise.

We paused.

"She has no wrinkles and owns an adorable baby goat!" I said, caught up in the moment. Two meatheads bench-pressing nearby turned to look.

Lisa shook her head, while I made a mental note to order more firming face crème.

It was energizing to think about dating with this deeper purpose in mind. This was different from setting a goal to *do* something or to *achieve* something. On our journeys Lisa and I desired to *become* something.

We agreed that every challenge, date, social experiment, conversation with a new guy, every competing moment—they'd all be rooted in the goal of becoming the best version of ourselves.

As we wiped down our gym equipment, conversation turned to birthdays and brunch. Like most Februarys, I felt excited about turning another year older, like a paintbrush hovering over a white canvas of endless potential.

"Speaking of birthdays," I said. "You're turning the big 3-0 in September. We need to plan something for you, Lis."

I could see her wheels begin to turn. Lisa was always meeting new people. We often joked that everyone from the nameless postal clerk to the flight attendant she'd likely never see again were among her best friends. While it wasn't often that she tied herself to any one group, she did have a tightknit community in Montana where she'd lived for three years before Idaho.

After thinking for a moment, she shared, "What if we take a sisters' camping trip to Glacier National Park? You, me, and Emily. Then do a big party with all my friends." The idea was the best of both her worlds: quality sister time followed by festivities with a group she absolutely loved.

I felt butterflies at the mention of a party with her Montana friends, though I did not say it out loud. *I wonder if I'll finally get to meet Evan.* The thought of meeting the guy Lisa had wanted to set me up with for four straight years made my heart stir.

But before I could get swept away by the what-ifs, Lisa had already moved on. "And we can also celebrate me winning the championship dating title," she said, pushing open the gym door. Cold air greeted us outside, but the Mile High City sun felt warm on my face.

"Keep dreaming, Lis." Just then, a drop of melted snow fell across my temple, like a wink from that old faithful tree. I looked up at its barren branches splitting across the clear blue sky. What a journey we had wintered together.

Driving probation was not the kick start I had wanted, yet it turned out to be exactly what I needed. During those six months, I dropped an entire pant size, resulting in more energy and fewer aches and pains. With my free time, I had hustled two jobs, cut expenses, and sold excess belongings, paying off over $10,000 in debt. Over time my home had become simpler, more breathable. And my soul did too.

As Lisa and I headed home to shower before brunch, we talked a mile a minute, designing the four categories we planned to compete in: Meet Men, First Dates, Level Up, and Couch-to-Marathon Training. It was a new year for me, a blank canvas, a fresh season that I couldn't wait to begin.

Chapter 3 | The Game Plan

Buttercup: We'll never survive.
Westley: Nonsense. You're only saying that because no one ever has.

~ The Princess Bride

Throughout March, Lisa and I put the finishing touches on our grand social experiment, leaving no stone left unturned.

We determined each dating challenge should be terrifying enough to stretch us but normal enough to keep us out of any future late-night *Girls Gone Wild* airings. Points varied depending on the challenge. The plan was to tally our earnings on a joint scoreboard via Zoom every Sunday.

At the end of six months, the winner would receive a $100 spa gift card—courtesy of the runner-up—and would also be crowned the Dating Champion of the World.

The four categories were as follows.

Category 1: Meet Men | 50 points

Meeting single men organically—in real life, not online—felt both important and intimidating. But our goal was bigger than awkwardly blurting out, "Hello," in the produce department followed by a victory dance in meats and deli.

We needed practice with *all the things*: striking up conversation, giving confident vibes, overcoming sweat mustaches, and offering guys a way to reach us if interested.

In order to earn 50 points, guys needed to meet three criteria, directly inspired by Dr. Henry Cloud's book:

1. They had to be new to us.
2. They must have had enough of an interaction with us to want to go out with us.
3. We must have provided enough info that they could follow through on that desire.

There was no rule saying we had to be interested in the guys. And they didn't even have to be interested in us. They did not have to prequalify as marriage material . . . and conversation didn't *have* to result with getting asked out.

Our only job was to practice winsome conversations and then provide enough information they could reach out if interested. Maybe that meant giving our number or chatting long enough to discover a mutual friend.

We wanted to create opportunities to observe ourselves, to reconnect with our emotions. To practice interacting. And to dig into the real insecurities, the *real* reasons we often felt stuck.

It was no accident this challenge earned the highest number of points. We knew it would require the most of us on an emotional level. If it wasn't worth 50 points, we'd avoid the discomfort altogether.

Category 2: First Dates | 25 points

Our new MO would be to go out with almost anyone, at least once. Unless, of course, they looked eerily similar to a guy on *America's Most Wanted*, or his mom drove him and waited in the car.

There was no rule on where to find dates. Online sites, setups by friends, or serendipitous meet-cutes were all fair game.

Historically, Lisa and I focused our first-date energy on two things: 1) assessing if the guy could be "the one" and 2) finding chemistry, that spark we longed for. It was always disappointing when dates lacked that special click and we'd have to start our search again. It was also a lot of pressure to put on a simple first date.

So, we decided to scrap the hunt for chemistry, at least temporarily. Our new focus would be on bringing our own A games, instead of worrying too much about theirs. For six months, dating would have little to do with who sat across from us, and more about becoming the date we hoped to find: confident and playful, generous and kind.

Category 3: Level Up | 10 points

Because our challenge was rooted in becoming better versions of ourselves, we brainstormed a list of healthy habits that could help us level up as singles too. To keep things simple, we selected three areas to focus on:

1. **Working Out**—Anything from simply getting fresh air on a gentle walk to elevating our heart rate at the gym would count. The goal? Movement. Releasing happy hormones. To stop living like baby sloths.
2. **Meeting with a Counselor/Mentor**—Pushing ourselves on a mental and emotional level was important to us. Having an outsider to process with and be accountable to felt like a wise move.

3. **Any Date, After the First**—While we planned to push ourselves to go on as many first dates as possible, we recognized healthy people give second chances and build connections. While exclusive relationships were off-limits during our competition, additional dates were not.

Category 4: Couch-to-Marathon Training | points vary monthly

When it came to putting ourselves out there, Lisa and I felt like two couch potatoes in desperate need of baby steps to get back in the race. To help, we planned to roll out a different theme each month, a checklist of goofy social experiments determined by the hurdles we needed to overcome.

Points would vary, and we'd be creating each flavor of the month along the way. Our hope was to keep the game playful, lighthearted, and fun. For our first month, April, our theme was called Conversation Starters, which featured a checklist of one-liners to help us break the ice with single guys.

Then There Was Kissing . . .

Yes, it's true. We created a no-kissing-for-six-months rule. But it wasn't because either of us didn't like kissing. Honestly, it was more because we do.

Going smooch free felt like inviting an entire diabetic support group to the candy store, then telling them they couldn't have any sweets. Crushing? Terribly. But we knew it was for our own good—and of the men we'd be dating, too, for that matter. Chocolate truffles and saltwater taffy are the best, but when you sample too many in a short amount of time, you end up not feeling very good.

Instead, we planned to take the Whole30 approach. Only, with our timeline it was more like the Whole183. Just like that trendy 30-day health plan helps participants temporarily trade problematic foods with the real, nutrient-dense stuff, we were curious how the same concept could impact our dating lives.

What would happen if we gave up the sweets (aka kissing) and focused on filling up on the wholesome, nutrient-packed ingredients of getting to know each other instead? To us, that meant creating meaningful connections with new guys and becoming the right women along the way.

What About Mr. Right?

There was, of course, the hope that our hard work would result in love. That raised the question: What happens if we meet our dream guy mid-challenge? Would we keep playing? Or would we be free to pursue a relationship?

That, we decided, would be part of the experiment. No matter how dreamy any guy was, we committed to a low simmer. Diving into exclusivity meant turning up the heat, but with 183 days ahead of us, we didn't want anyone getting burned.

If our main goal was finding the right person, dropping out for Mr. Right made sense. Yet while we *hoped* to meet a great guy, our *goal* was becoming the right person.

If Mr. Right magically showed up, we could totally go on more dates, just in a simmer sort of way.

Accountability

"I'm going to need a first-date outfit," I blurted matter-of-factly. It was the last Sunday in March and our final Zoom before the competition began.

Without looking up, I scribbled fast and furious into my notebook. Lisa sat on the other side of the screen, feet propped, not a care in the world.

I was the person whose stress levels were consoled by checking things off a list. What I couldn't bring myself to say out loud was, *I'm scared of being terrible at this. I've never walked up to a cute guy before and struck up conversation out of thin air, unless I'm in line at Chipotle placing an order for a burrito bowl.*

But Lisa, my extroverted counterpart, flew through life by the seat of her pants and didn't read between my lines.

"Okay, go for it," she shrugged.

"I'm also going to need the monthly point systems printed and a copy in each pocket, purse, and wallet that I own." Smokestacks poured from my pen.

"Wow," Lisa said, staring at me like I was an alien baby.

"I'll need Kleenex boxes in case things don't go well . . ."

"Yes, that's probably true."

"We're going to need a top-secret shareable Google doc . . ."

"What?"

"To record every detail of our points and feelings and emotions and victories and learning experiences." (Deep breath.) "And Lis?"

"Yes, Jen?"

"You know when you see lovers' names carved into a tree? I don't think that's cute. I just find it strange how many people have knives on a date."

"That is both insightful and weird."

"Thanks. I read it on Pinterest this morning. But for real, do you think we should have some sort of safety playbook? We could call it the '7 Habits of Highly Successful Daters'!" I said, sweeping my palm across the air.

"Yes. We should absolutely have a safety playbook. But let's call it the 'Don't Get Killed Agreement,'" she shot back.

And that's how we decided to create the "7 Habits of Highly Effective Daters Who Don't Get Killed" pact. It read as follows.

From April 1 through September 30, we hereby promise to:

- Drive ourselves to dates and only hang out in public places.
- Text someone beforehand to let them know where we'll be.
- Go out with almost anyone, at least once. But don't accept questionable or weirdo dates solely for points.
- Uphold a self-given 10:30 p.m. curfew, to ensure good life decisions are made.
- Ditch the husband-hunt mentality and focus on getting to know ourselves.
- Practice a Whole183, nutrient-packed, "sugar-free" challenge.
- Meet via video chat every Sunday for accountability, scoreboard updates, and encouragement.

Virtual Blood Pact

On March 31, the day before our adventure commenced, I emailed Lisa a shared Google doc containing the agreement and a chart to track our points. We both signed in red Times New Roman—a virtual blood pact.

And just like that, the creation of our competition was complete. I knew the easy part was behind us; it was my fears of what would come next that had me smoking three packs of invisible cigarettes a day. Nothing like a drag of quality air to quiet the mind.

That night, I hung my pressed business clothes on the door. My brows were freshly waxed and accessories carefully chosen. My laptop and work training materials were prepped and packed. And I had rehearsed every Conversation Starter on our list.

Then, like an addict the night before she's about to get sober, I curled into an introverted ball on the couch in front of my crackling fireplace and watched another rom-com on my laptop, alone, for the thousandth time.

As the final credits rolled, I reached for my phone: 12:02 a.m. *Fool's Day*. I smiled. The dating challenge had officially begun.

Chapter 4 | Conversation Starters

"I see you're drinking 1 percent. Is that because you think you're fat? Because you're not. You could be drinking whole if you wanted to."

~ *Napoleon breaking the ice with Deb,* Napoleon Dynamite

Day 1 | Standing dead center aisle, somewhere between the frozen tots and fudgsicles, I tightened my grip around the red plastic grocery cart handle. My eyes rested with the delicacy of laser beams on my first targeted bachelor at the end of the freezer section.

Curled in my right hand was a printed list of thirty conversation starters. Roughly the size of an index card, it was still gummy from the glue stick I used to adhere a blue construction paper border before leaving the house. Because I'm seven like that.

The gentleman possessed everything I needed in a target. He was ringless, alone, hygienically suitable, and of similar age. And after a jam-packed workday teaching facial protocols to fifteen women at a local day spa, he was also the first man I'd seen all day.

Staring through the frosted glass case, the bachelor was unsuspecting and unaware of the turmoil his presence was causing. *It's not like I've never talked to a guy before,* I thought, creeping the squeaky wheels of my metal cart toward him. *Why does this feel so weird?* In hindsight, the sneaking and creeping might have had something to do with it.

According to our guidelines, Lisa and I had thirty days to use the list of predetermined one-liners on thirty new single guys. Each icebreaker earned 10 points, with the potential for 50 bonus points to whoever completed the entire list.

Each line was designed to help us ease into the game; it was no secret we were feeling a bit sluggish when it came to putting ourselves out there.

For Lisa it was the hurdle of small-town living. She was an outgoing youth director living in rural Idaho, where the population teetered around eight thousand. Everyone, it seemed, was married, in grade school, or a decade into social security. (Believe me, you haven't seen a slim dating pool until you've checked out Hinge in a one-stoplight town.)

As for me, I was more introverted—though not really shy—a needle in a haystack buried in a metro population of over three million. I was rusty when it came to striking up conversation with men. And while I tended to blame my busy schedule, the deeper truth was after years of not practicing, I simply didn't know how.

But neither of us wanted to let those hurdles get in our way. We recognized the genesis to every love story had one thing in common: somebody started the conversation. Someone said the first hello. Someone offered a nervous handshake paired with "Hi, you must be [insert name]; It's nice to finally meet you." Perhaps one bumped into another, apologizing.

Successes began with that infamous "Don't I know you from somewhere?" Other champs awkwardly made their way across a room, blurting out whatever came to mind: "I like your [sweater, shoes, biceps, receding hairline, lips, cankles]." All we knew was that there was power in knowing how to start the opening act.

Parking my cart next to single-frozen-food-section guy, I felt my mouth go dry. I had preselected Conversation Starter #3 from the list, created specifically for meeting single men in stores. Just a simple "Hey! Have you tried either of these? Which do you recommend?" But instead of executing, I found myself staring at him in silence for more Mississippis than I'd like to own up to. He glanced up, startled.

In my mind the line would be flirty but not over the top. Just enough to break the ice. To practice striking up conversation with confidence and on cue. If things went well, I even considered throwing in a confident hair flip. But instead of a cute-girl "Hey!" I heard myself let out a deep, weighty "Hhhhh-iiiiiiii," fogging up the cool glass case in front of us. While I can't be certain, I think my eyes crossed too.

Unbroken silence followed. It was as thick and bottomless as the regret that washed over me realizing I never should have sampled that new garlic dip in aisle 9 before making my big move.

Without response, the bachelor shot a hopeful glance over his shoulder, uncertain if I was talking to him. Turning back, he swallowed and paused. Then he tossed his frozen beef patties into his cart and wheeled away.

Whether the shutdown was due to my gawky presence or my fatal mistake in aisle 9, I may never know. What I do know is that instead of brushing myself off and looking for another bachelor, I drove home and sank into the safety of my comfort zone, dreaming of someday. A day when I would magically wake up as a less awkward, awkward person.

Beginner's Luck

Day 2 | "Guess who used Conversation Starter #4 at a coffee shop today?" Lisa texted. I was in the middle of a slice of leftover pizza, tucked inside for the evening wearing sweats at half past six. Staring at the message, I grabbed my purse and pulled out the checklist, running my finger down the card until I hit her line: "4) Excuse me, do you mind helping me with something?"

Before I could respond, another text came through.

"I gave my cell number to Jeff. He's the barista."

And another . . .

"I also went to the gym this morning!"

Then another . . .

"I think I'm going to sign up for eHarmony tonight too."

She ended the text stream with, "How was your day?"

I looked at the mess of scissors, markers, paper clippings, and glue sticks littered across the kitchen table, leftover from Day 1's craft session. My new driver's license revealed I was in my midthirties. So why did I suddenly feel sixteen in dating years?

"Wow, great job, Lis!" I texted back with forced enthusiasm. "I've had a busy day. I'll get out there tomorrow." I decided to leave off that by "busy" I meant I wasn't really feeling it and by "tomorrow" I meant maybe never. Pausing, I ended with, "So, your phone number, huh? Did this Jeff guy ask you for it?"

She responded with a short recap of her morning. After asking Jeff if she could hang her Young Life posters on the community board, she chatted with him for ten minutes, then gave him a poster with her name and cell number written on it, in case he wanted to reach her.

Dang, I thought, rereading the texts. Lisa made it sound so easy.

My mind wandered back to earlier that same morning. I was also at a coffee shop, sitting two tables away from a single guy working on his laptop. My mind had raced, determined to select the perfect line from our list.

Number 7, "What a cute dog! What's his name?" wouldn't work on the canineless bachelor. Number 14, "Would you mind helping me carry these?" would only make me look like an idiot, considering I had a purse and a coffee carafe. I couldn't do number 10, "Can you spot me on this machine?" There was no bench press in sight.

So instead of trying something, anything, I did nothing. Which brought the Day 2 scoreboard to Lisa, 80 points, and Jen, zero.

Meh, she's probably just having beginner's luck, I reassured myself, taking another bite of cold pizza.

Little did I know those two days of excuses would turn into four. And four days would turn into eight. And eight days would turn into sixteen. *Maybe tomorrow,* I kept saying.

Until suddenly it was Day 21, and I still hadn't checked off a single Conversation Starter.

Compartmentalized Confidence

Day 21 | Settling into the deep leather couch cushions in my new counselor's office, I surveyed the room. There was a rubbery green floor plant by a large picture window, shaded by willow trees. A rich mahogany desk sat to my left, a matching corner curio cabinet to my right. There was a wall of framed, important-looking certificates.

My counselor sat, legs crossed, in a plush armchair, wearing a starched white blouse and smiling over emerald-green readers that rested on the lower bridge of her nose. Everything looked exactly how I imagined it based on the images that popped up during my Google search for "Christian counselors near me."

If you must know, this was my first non-workout-inspired points of the challenge, so *ding!* Congratulations to me. Sure, I hadn't tried a single Conversation Starter yet. Nor had I given any men my contact info. Nor had I gone on any dates.

I had, however, worked out eight whole times, which averaged out to be 2.67 workouts per week. According to the FDA, I was 0.33 workouts short of a healthy lifestyle, and according to the scoreboard, I was roughly 33 million workouts away from catching up to Lisa.

Meanwhile in Idaho, my competition had given her info to a handful of single softball coaches at a high school away game she attended the night before. Needless to say, Lisa did not possess "beginner's luck" as I'd first hoped. I guess she just had actual luck, or maybe skill, or possibly superpowers, or something I clearly did not have.

"So, tell me what brings you in today, Jen."

"Of course." I nodded, all business.

I explained to my new counselor I was currently in last place of a dating competition that I myself created, and there was a very important fictitious championship title plus an invisible fake crown at stake here. Her eyes widened, then blinked several times before scribbling some sort of notes onto a legal pad.

Six minutes later, she stopped writing. "Go on."

"I think I have a debilitating case of 'compartmentalized confidence,'" I explained.

Compartmentalized confidence was what I had nicknamed my unique combination of abilities and inabilities. I was self-assured when training adult learners how to properly release the sternocleidomastoid, masseter, and orbicularis oculi facial muscles. But I lacked that same smooth operator mentality and sparkle when tasked with meeting single men in our competition.

Confidence spilled over when I directed technical workshops, led church small groups, hosted men and women in my home, or mentored teens. I was a comfortable conversationalist, able to shoot the breeze with most anyone. Yet weaving through a room to approach a new guy? I was a total flight risk.

"There's another problem too," I said. "Guys don't really notice me. Actually, let me rephrase that. Normal guys don't really notice me."

Just the day prior, I was walking into the grocery store when I heard a male voice behind me say, "Hey there, sugar, wanna lift?" When I turned around, there was a man with wiry silver hair pushing a grocery cart my way. To make matters worse, the silver hair wasn't on his shiny bald head; it was coming out of his nose. And his ears, too, for that matter.

I thought perhaps he was offering a funny grandpa joke until he asked if I'd consider going on a date with him. For 25 points, the thought crossed my mind. But then I remembered:

A. Lisa and I agreed not to go on weirdo dates solely for points.

B. Also, I would rather die.

"It's like my spirit animal, George Costanza, once said," I said matter-of-factly, "'When I like them, they don't like me. And when they like me, I don't like them.'"

Instead of handing me a box of tissues and mug of cocoa, my counselor glanced at her watch and said, "Well, that concludes today's session. You have three homework assignments before I see you next month." She handed me an invoice. "That will be $100 please. Cash or card?"

Three homework assignments? One sounded sufficient, but I bit my tongue. "I'll pay cash."

Lisa had scored a mentor: an older woman at her church who didn't give homework and cost nothing, plus—bonus—bought her donuts. Once again, it seemed Lisa had all the luck.

My heart tightened as I handed over five precious twenty dollars bills, picturing the dent they could have made on my debt snowball. Then I wrote down my assignments.

First, I had to join an online dating site and email five guys who seemed to be what I was looking for. Even if I didn't think they would return the interest.

Next, I was instructed to watch a TED Talk by Amy Cuddy titled "Your Body Language May Shape Who You Are."

Lastly, I was told to repeat the phrase "fake it till you become it" every single day, a twist on the old fake-it-till-you-make-it adage. She said the TED Talk would explain more on that.

As we stood, she said, "You're more confident than you give yourself credit for. Just think of yourself as practicing what you already are, in an area of your life that you're currently not. You'll get there."

Excuses

Driving home, I reflected on her words. We were three weeks into the competition, and I trailed Lisa by over 400 points. My probation glow-up had faded fast, and *making room* now felt like a distant memory.

Work was ramping up, and I had gladly quit my second job. One of the spa workshops I created, "90-Second Skin Care," was earning lots of national attention. Marketing pieces I'd made for another class were also circulating around spas outside my region. Professionally, it was such an exciting time, and I felt so happy my hard work was paying off.

But when it came to everything else—the dating challenge, working out, eating healthy meals in, hustling my debt—I felt like I was losing ground. And instead of leaning in, I found myself backing out.

In March and April, the numbers on my scale had started to sneak back up. Restaurant spending increased 226 percent over my monthly average during probation. Gym visits slowed. Momentum on my debt-freedom plan had too.

When it came to starting our competition, I suppose there was a part of me that assumed a swirl of magic fairy dust would settle over me on April 1, brightening my charm and tightening my pores. But clearly that joke was on me.

Instead, I was clinging to a truckload of excuses, each one starting with *someday* and *right after* and *maybe when . . .*

Someday I'll be ready to start this thing.

Maybe when I'm in better shape, then I can compete against Lisa.

Right after this fiscal year ends sounds like a better launch date. Speaking of being busy with work, what's a few weeks of takeout going to hurt?

Maybe a makeover or new wardrobe is what I need to boost my confidence. I could pause my debt-freedom goal for a while. Giving myself a couple extra months or even another year really makes more sense.

Before starting our competition, Lisa and I had created a list of excuses that often held us back as singles. I could feel myself clinging to a handful of those too:

- I'll put myself out there when I . . . *feel more confident, meet the right person, get in shape, find a guy who makes the first move, have more energy.*
- Maybe someday I won't . . . *feel so intimidated to say hello, be this busy, still be stuck on the one that got away.*
- I'll start dating right after . . . *this month, this Hulu series ends. Definitely-maybe it's a possibility in the New Year.*

We wrote them down, knowing the list might come in as a handy reminder to keep going if we hit plateaus. I just didn't think I'd hit one so fast.

Turning my car into my apartment complex parking lot, I saw my tall, dark, handsome neighbor sliding planks of wood across his table saw in front of his building. Stacks of 4x4's mingled with bags of Miracle-Gro across the manicured lawn.

Everything inside me begged to climb the four flights of stairs to my apartment. Yet deep down, I heard that familiar whisper. *Make room.*

Make room for confidence, for courage, for dating, for becoming that best version of yourself.

Make room.

Neighbor McHottie

Parking my car, I turned off the ignition and gripped the wheel at ten and two. In the rearview mirror, McHottie worked away, his brow sweat glistening in the Denver sun.

Reaching into my purse, I pulled out the Conversation Starter cheat sheet. It was clear that my dating life could be summed up by that blue-bordered list. I was the queen of masterfully crafted plans and detailed blueprints for future success, yet always stuck waiting for the conditions in my life to be just right before I could begin.

Until now.

Pausing on #12, I read it out loud, not once but twice. *It's perfect,* I thought, then read it a third and a fourth time for good measure. And whispered it a fifth and a sixth with my eyes closed, just to make sure.

Stepping out of my car, my shoes hit a sheet of ice, leftover in the shadows of my building despite the warm April day. My body flung wildly this way and that, hanging by only a car door handle, until I finally steadied myself and stood facing the row of townhomes across the pavement.

With one fierce pull, I hiked up my Spanx, snapping them into place, then stepped out of the shadows toward McHottie. My confidence could catch up with me when it was ready.

You survived Black Friday in children's clothing, I reminded myself as I took a step with my right foot. *Your new Golden Prism lip shine is like a force field of magnetic powers.* I moved my left foot forward. *You possess the elegance and strength of a white Bengal tiger.* I stepped with my right foot again.

But the closer I got, the louder the voices of perfectionism became.

You don't have to subject yourself to this humiliation, you know.

Fifty bucks he likes petite blondes with crystal-blue eyes, a small pore size, and an expansive baking repertoire.

May I point out that you have premature grays and mismatched socks?

My right foot edged off the asphalt and onto his lawn; my left followed. He looked up from the table saw, his chiseled forearms kissed with just the right amount of sawdust. He reeked of manliness. I reeked of uncertainty with a hint of breakfast burrito.

"Hey there. Can I help you?" he said, brushing strands of adorable brown curls away from his brow.

I decided to kick things off with a bold and highly advanced move: The Flirtatious Ponytail Swing. In synchronized slow motion, I tossed my head back and forth as my hair took to the breeze and I announced my line. There was just one tiny problem. Only an amateur would attempt a flirtatious ponytail swing while wearing a thick glossy coat of Golden Prism lip shine.

"Looks [*thhhptttt*] like quite [*thhhpppptttt*] the project. What are you working on?" I said, pulling sticky strands from my lips.

The corner of his mouth tugged in amusement; then he began an in-depth mansplanation of his task. I was promptly lost, both by the word "torques" and a new dilemma that burned inside.

Sure, I'd earned 10 points for checking Conversation Starter #12 off the list. But now, in order to earn my first 50 pointer, I had to give the gentleman a way to contact me if he was interested.

The situation was teed up to perfection.

Step 1) Simply state my name.

Step 2) Point to Unit 329 across the street so he knew where to find me.

But as he wrapped up Woodworking 101, silence crept between us. I froze. Those punk inner voices rumbled inside me, and I felt my toes edge toward the asphalt.

"Well, nice talking to you," I blurted, bringing our conversation to a hard, fast end. Maybe if I held onto my name and way to find me, failure or rejection weren't possible outcomes.

"Have a good day." He nodded, then bent down to pick up another plank of wood from the pile by his feet.

I turned, retreating toward home. In that moment, I couldn't help but wonder if maybe it wasn't Lisa I was competing against after all.

As his table saw buzzed back to life, my counselor's words rushed through me. *You're more confident than you give yourself credit for. Just think of yourself as practicing what you already are, in an area of your life that you're currently not. You'll get there.*

Chapter 5 | PRFCT4U

Stan Fields: Ms. Rhode Island, please describe your idea of a perfect date.
Cheryl "Ms. Rhode Island": That's a tough one. I'd have to say April 25th.
Because it's not too hot, not too cold, all you need is a light jacket.

~ Ms. Congeniality

Day 22 | It was a nice sentiment and all, realizing fear was a bigger threat to my dating game than Lisa was. But the clock was ticking and I refused to let the scoreboard go up in flames.

That night I joined Match and Christian Mingle, then texted Lisa my profile screenshots with the caption "Game on." While she was new to online dating, it wasn't my first rodeo. And after surveying my next five and a half months' worth of options, I prayed it was my last.

"At what point does a man decide his absolute best profile photo is in the bathroom mirror without a shirt on?" I text-ranted to Lisa. "It's like a third of these guys just woke up from a post-NFL nap, ripped a loud beer belch to relieve the bloat, walked into the bathroom, and snapped an impromptu mirror selfie."

She responded with a laughing emoji. I followed with a skull and crossbones.

Truth be told, I'd experienced some real doozie online dates in my day. There was the guy who took me, play by play, through forty solid minutes of his personal tractor-pulling competition videos. Followed by a thirty-minute slideshow of each trophy he'd ever won. I can't remember if that was before or after he fried up some fish without dinner plates, napkins, or utensils, serving piping hot greasy filets directly into my awkwardly cupped hands.

Then there was the gentleman who slammed his three-fingered left hand onto the dinner table in a fine dining establishment, so loudly that heads around us turned. "Bet you're wondering how this chain saw massacre happened!" he shouted, right as I took a bite of my honey-seared chicken.

I could go on, but I'll stop there.

In addition to my apprehension of the potential jokers I'd be meeting online, there was also the competition. My friend Katrina had recently shown me the women we were up against on a new dating app she was on. "Gosh," I'd commented, "It's like an endless stream of hot yoga babes with bottomless mani budgets, trendy boho lofts, daily collagen habits, and beachy travel blogs."

My profile felt basic next to theirs. I guess that's what happens when your last exotic vacation was to rural Idaho.

But I was determined to give it my best shot. Following my counselor's assignment, I began narrowing my search, preparing to message five men with qualities I was looking for. Like a drive-through value meal, anything was customizable.

There was height, body type, interests, and hobbies. Religion, education, views on kids, income range. Were they single, currently separated, divorced, or widowed? There were preferred pets, favorite reads, TV shows. You could click favorite sports to watch and sports played. Smoking habits, drinking habits, vacation preferences. And, of course, the "About Me" section—your chance to freestyle it.

Leaning back in my chair, I stared at the screen. *So, what type of guy am I looking for?* My mind wandered to Evan, Lisa's friend in Montana. We'd never met, but after four years of Lisa's stories, I felt like we had.

According to her, Evan was my perfect match. She had spent several years talking me up to him—and talking him up to me. Naturally, I had done my own research too. I admit that on more than one occasion, I'd scouted his social profiles, feeling more certain each time that we would totally hit it off. Based on everything Lisa had told me about him, he was everything I hoped was still out there. He had every box on my list checked.

A man of faith, a family man, and of course, tall. A strong businessman, witty, sharp with words. A mentor, community volunteer, outdoorsy but not hard-core. Kind to the elderly, good at networking, and perhaps with a little less baggage many had at our age.

Plans were underway for Lisa's thirtieth birthday in September—our sister's adventure trip to Glacier National Park. Camping and hiking were on our list. And so was that big bash for Lisa with all her closest friends. While Emily and I promised to take care of party planning, Lisa's eyes had danced: "And I'll take care of setting up you and Evan."

Maybe I had watched a few too many rom-coms, or perhaps I felt like only God could ordain such a well-timed story. Either way, it did not feel like luck that I would be meeting Evan in the final weeks of our dating competition. By all my interpretations, this was destiny.

That night, I input my criteria on Match and Christian Mingle, then emailed five men with qualities I looked for. I can't say there was anyone I was all that excited about. To be honest, the lineup felt like warm-ups before the end-of-summer big game. But putting in the work and pushing myself toward growth were still real-time goals. No matter what September held regarding Evan, I planned to do everything in my power to catch up to Lisa. Maybe even pull into the lead.

Yet more than winning the dating competition, I wanted to win at love. Deep down, there was a flicker I dared not whisper out loud. A small, quiet hope that when Emily, Lisa, and I ventured to Glacier in five months, maybe, just maybe, my search would finally be over.

Responses

The next morning, I was encouraged to find exactly five new messages in my inboxes. Pouring myself a cup of coffee, I sat down at my kitchen table and logged in to both accounts, excited to see who'd replied. As I scrolled the messages, it didn't take long to realize none of the original men had responded.

Instead, I received these:

> **PRFCT4U:** Tell me those eyes come with GPS, Jen, because I'm already getting lost . . .

> **VIETNAMVET11:** Dang. I think you should find short, older men attractive!

> **SETH83:** Hi. I enjoyed reading your profile. And I really like your photos. Im writing you, to ask you, if you will marry me? Im writing you to ask, if I can take you as my wife. I want to take you as my wife. I want to marry you. And Im willing to do whatever it takes for your hand in marriage. Please let me know, what I need to do, to take your hand, in marriage. – Seth Robustelli

> **MATCHGUY99:** Hey Veronica! That is great you're able to spend lots of time with your family. It looks like you have two brothers? Espresso is pretty stout; I don't drink it that much. How was your week? Do you have any weekend plans? Nice to hear from you. Have a great weekend! – Tim

> **MATCHGUY99:** Sorry Jen. As you probably noticed I meant to send an email to Veronica, not you. – Tim

Staring at the screen, I didn't know whether to die laughing or to crawl back into bed, pull the covers over my head, and accept destiny by binge-adopting stray cats from every shelter website in the tristate region. The internet had always been one more reminder the odds were good, but the goods were definitely odd.

Taking a deep breath, I decided to let impulse lead. Hitting reply on one of the messages, I typed the following:

Dear Seth Robustelli,

Sure. Why not.

Sincerely, Jen

Homework

Day 26 | Three days later, I arrived at a new restaurant, rallying for my first date of the competition. He wasn't one of my initial five; I had yet to hear from any of them. And no, it wasn't crazy Seth Robustelli either.

He found me on Match and, according to his photos, was going to be a hybrid lumberjack slash oil-rigging engineer. Steel-blue eyes. A thick brown beard. Flannelled broad shoulders against a rugged mountain backdrop. To which I promptly replied, *Yes, please.*

Beyond photos, it was tough to gauge our compatibility. Like many guys, his profile and emails resembled a man of few words and littler description. But according to competition rules, my assessment of him was not the purpose for our date. I was there to practice being the dater I hoped to find.

Walking into the restaurant, I felt nervous for at least eleven reasons. But with only a few minutes before his ETA, I only had time to think about one.

"Excuse me, where's the women's restroom?" I asked the seating hostess. She pointed toward the back, near the kitchen, and I thanked her. *Here goes nothing*, I thought, weaving in and out of tables.

Locking myself in a dimly lit stall, I stood, feet planted. Squaring my shoulders, I threw my arms up into the air as if I'd just crossed the Boston Marathon finish line. Then I started counting.

One. Two. Three. Four . . .

It was called "power posing," as seen in my second homework assignment, Amy Cuddy's TED Talk called "Your Body Language May Shape Who You Are." I wanted to bring my A game, and I was willing to try anything.

Just then, the restroom door opened. Heels clacked across the tile, pausing in front of my stall. Everything from my forearms to my fingertips poked above the door like two old-school TV antennas stretching for a signal.

Hey there! I wanted to wave. *Nothing like a little first date prep as part of your counselor's homework, am I right, girlfriend?* Yet something about that statement sounded worse than anonymous silence. I refrained.

Forty-eight. Forty-nine. Fifty. Fifty-one . . .

My neighbor's toilet flushed, and she exited to wash her hands. I held my pose, noting all blood had drained from my fingertips, pooling into my shoulders. I reassured myself numb arms were a small price to pay for the confidence boost I'd gain from my exciting new pregame warm-up.

In her TED Talk, Amy Cuddy explained how body language had the power to elevate confidence, warmth, engagement, and attraction. Done right, it could increase chances for new jobs, work promotions, even dates. Her TED Talk ranked as one of the most watched of all time. Needless to say, I was listening.

To test her "power posing" theory, her research team gave half their participants high-power poses to hold, like my finish-line victory arms, the Wonder Woman pose, or sitting reclined with an arm casually slung around a neighboring chair. Other participants were given low-power poses: a variety of rolled shoulders, shy postures, and guarded limbs.

Each person's saliva was tested beforehand, then retested two minutes after the experiment. Samples were analyzed for testosterone levels (the power hormone) and cortisol levels (the stress hormone).

Results were staggering. Power hormones skyrocketed in people holding high-power poses; there were significant drops in their stress hormones too. Those who held low-power poses had the opposite effect: lowered testosterone and elevated cortisol.

One hundred and seventeen. One hundred and eighteen. One hundred and nineteen . . .

Just then, I heard my phone *ding!* as a new text came through. *One hundred and twenty.* I breathed, dropping my arms to my sides. They had a weird feeling, like when you wake up in the middle of the night to a random arm in your bed and scream, only to pick it up and realize it's your own arm that's fallen asleep.

Grabbing my phone, I read the text from my date. *I'm here.* Time to see if power posing had paid off.

Practice Makes Confidence

First-date introductions are always a little odd. One person goes in for a hug, the other for a handshake. Or there's the canoe-paddle-length, long-distance smile, ending with one person reaching out for a side hug while the other mistakes it for a high five.

That night was no different. I will never forget the sheer terror as my arms buzzed with full-force pins and needles when my date and I attempted our first point of contact. Let's just say some version of a hug happened, and one of us almost gave the other a black eye. In hindsight, fully functioning arms would have been a nice touch.

My date was handsome. I gave him four out of five stars on the profile accuracy chart, docking him for claiming he was six feet when he was not a hair over five ten. His conversation skills, on the other hand, were dull as a butter knife. But I reminded myself I wasn't there to analyze his five-star rating. It was an opportunity to assess mine.

For the rest of dinner, I practiced a variety of other, more discreet power poses. Shoulders rolled back, uncrossed arms. Kind facial expressions. Voicing thoughtful questions, inserting confident answers.

As I did, I wondered what my body language had communicated before. Like when I slunk behind the guy in the frozen food section, or when I was sitting near the coffee shop bachelor, with whom I never even tried. And of course, when I approached neighbor McHottie.

According to the TED Talk, improving body language wasn't about scoring the promotion, attracting a partner, or owning the spotlight. I learned power posing had less to do with altering how others viewed me. The ultimate goal was to upgrade the message I was sending to myself.

After paying for dinner, my date walked me to my car. I had the sneaking suspicion he was expecting a good-night kiss. Something about the way he lingered at my door, his eyes staring at my lips while we talked.

But Lisa and I had committed to a Whole30, sugar-free challenge. We desired to meet a large variety of guys and, even more importantly, to better ourselves. Diving in, lips first, would only be a distraction.

I thanked him for the evening, and we hugged (thank you, fully functioning arms), then said good night. We never did kiss, and he never did call. Both were fine with me.

Showing Up, Badly

Whether Lisa was getting lazy or perhaps a little too cocky, I may never know. But in the last few days of April, my score crept up behind hers.

The hype sent me on a text-a-thon tailspin, blowing up her phone with "Booyah!" and "#scoreboard" and emojis of every trophy and medal I could get my hot little hands on. Yes, I was constantly slobbering all over my words. But I was doing the work, and it was starting to show.

During April's weekly Zoom meetings, I took strong mental notes as Lisa revealed her successes. Gutsy and bold, if that girl feared rejection, she never showed it.

"I just walked up to him at the restaurant, held out my hand, and said Conversation Starter #11. 'Hi! I'm Lisa. That looks really good. What are you having?'"

An hour later, she dropped a big stack of mail in front of a single guy at the post office. *On purpose.* Flashing her doe eyes, she asked Conversation Starter #15, "Would you mind giving me a hand?" By the time they parted ways, she had given him her phone number for an extra 50 points.

But it wasn't just her confidence that inspired me to push myself outside my comfort zone. There was the simple fact I refused to lose to that turkey. In the last three days of April, I started spitting out Conversation Starters with the grace and class of a string of sumo wrestlers performing at Disney on Ice.

Like when I spotted a guy doing post-workout stretches on a corner mat at the gym. Plopping myself down, I blurted out Conversation Starter #5: "I think I've seen you around here before! I'm Jen." At least, that's how the line was supposed to go.

Instead, my voice carried a weird Tarzan vibe: "Me seen you here." (Insert barbaric fist pound on chest.) "Me Jen." Awkward does not begin to describe the moments that followed, so we can slowly back away from that story.

Then there was Espresso Guy, a gentleman standing at a coffee bar waiting for his Americano one afternoon. In my eagerness to not let any opportunities for points pass me by, I leaped from my cozy couch spot and headed his way, shimmying in and out of tall tables and bar stools, spinning in weird triple-axel-type moves.

Within seconds I crashed into one of the tables, causing a disastrous domino effect. Landing, breathless, inches from my targeted bachelor, I announced Conversation Starter #2 with a big lopsided grin: "I love your hat!" To my surprise, he didn't run for the door. Instead, he returned the big silly grin and thanked me.

It was obvious either my catastrophic nosedive or winded compliment really made his day. My performance ended with, "Okay then," and us parting ways. Despite my maniac tendencies, I felt pretty good about the whole thing. Making his day really made mine.

Conversations ended as quickly as they started, making the task of getting past the one-liners as tough as the gym felt the previous September. That first fall date with the elliptical lasted only seventeen minutes.

Yes, I'd been out of shape. But the harder pill to swallow was the only way to create change was to continue showing up badly.

Again.

And again.

And again.

And again.

Thirty-four weeks of showing up badly to the gym were behind me, and those first seventeen minutes that felt like climbing Everest while pulling a sled of Ford F150s were now a simple warm-up.

I prayed the same principles that applied to my waistline also applied to my dating game. So, I vowed to keep showing up, even if it was badly.

Comfort Zone

A lot had happened since April Fool's Day, now a month behind us. I couldn't put my finger on it, but something felt different.

While I loved the safety of my comfort zone, I was realizing I'd overstayed my welcome. Too much time buried in life's pillows and wrapped in its cotton sheets had left me a bit sluggish. Getting up felt more like a stumble than a walk down the hall. Yes, I loved my comfort zone. I just didn't love the side effects.

The alarm clock? Killer. The lights? Too bright. And it's cold when feet leave the sheets and hit the hard floor. But after four weeks of a new routine, I was starting to see everything I'd been missing out on staying in my comfort zone. Playing it safe, keeping warm.

Past the cold floors were sunrises, coffees, a walk, or a run. And that's where I now stood—hating the cruelty of the hardwood with everything in me, yet realizing that maybe, just maybe, there was something more beyond the open door.

Chapter 6 | Venues

"I can't go out tonight (fake coughs). I'm sick."

~ *Karen Smith,* Mean Girls

Leaning against my kitchen counter on the first Saturday morning in May, I yawned, still groggy from a late night of typing up the final details for a Venues Challenge, our new monthly theme.

While Conversation Starters encouraged us to meet more guys, we realized there weren't always guys in the places we routinely went. Trying to find bachelors in the Magnolia aisles at Target was like showing up for tennis practice at the soccer field. It was tough to volley a ball when there was no one to return the serve.

Just then my phone buzzed, interrupting my thoughts. "Swung by the farmer's market. Gave two single guys my number."

"Oh, for Pete's sake." I rolled my eyes behind an old pair of over-sized tortoise frames. Still in my slippers and sweats, I was barely halfway through my first cup of coffee. Meanwhile, Lisa was on her own personal rocket ship, soaring toward the championship title and $100 prize money.

Of course that stinker is bright eyed and bushy tailed, I groaned. She wasn't the one who added our entire list of eighty-two venue ideas into our shared Google doc the previous night. To help kick-start the month, we had brainstormed new places to meet single guys:

Attend a charity gala or new art gallery opening. Go to a conference, try a networking group. Take a bike maintenance workshop, sign up for fly-fishing lessons. Film festivals and farmer's markets. Auto shows and live music.

We weren't limited to the list of eighty-two ideas; we could get creative too. In order to earn 10 points for a new venue, it required three qualifiers; it had to be a place

1. where we didn't ordinarily go,
2. where there were people we were not ordinarily with,
3. with the goal and intention of meeting new single guys.

That kept things flexible enough for Lisa, living in a small rural community. Denver had a zillion options fitting that description. My biggest hurdle would involve snuffing out my invisible smokes, strapping on my seat belt, and going to them.

According to Lisa's text, she hadn't wasted a single second diving in. Instead of responding to her message, I called.

"Hey," she picked up casually.

"Spill," I said, swallowing my remaining coffee in one long, desperate chug.

"You're going to love this one, Jen." Even without video, I knew there was a twinkle in her eyes.

That morning, Lisa drove to a farmer's market in a neighboring town. Instead of perusing the produce, she was on a mission to find single guys. Within minutes, she spotted two eligibles selling a variety of homemade dog foods and treats. Walking over, she started asking genuine questions about their products, how they got into business, what their company vision was, etc.

"You could totally tell the guys were getting super excited. Like they were getting closer and closer to the biggest sale of their careers." By this point, Lisa was laughing so hard she could barely talk. "Then, one of them asked what kind of dog I have . . ."

There was silence on the line. I knew it wasn't for dramatic effect. When Lisa starts laughing, tears and the inability to speak aren't far behind. Growing up, she was regularly excused from dinner to do some deep breathing. Regaling her own stories always put Lisa into absolute stitches.

Shaking my head, I waited while she pulled herself together.

"I was like, 'Oh, well, I don't have a dog,'" she continued through tears.

I guess the guys looked pretty stunned as she winked at them, her motives becoming clear. With their jaws on the ground, she gave them her contact information, in case they were ever interested. Then she pulled out her wallet and bought a big bag of dog treats for her nonexistent dog.

"You still bought something?" I was laughing now, too, dying to know what had happened next.

I could almost hear her shrug as she wiped away tears. "I just walked away, sporting my Super Mario Brothers T-shirt and carrying the huge bag of dog treats home to my imaginary pup."

Lisa was so over-the-top, so next level, and I loved her for it. Yet it was difficult to imagine a day where I would pull ahead of her in our challenge. I hated losing. I hated losing in love, I hated losing in superficial dating competitions, and I hated losing my mind. But there I was again, folks, losing all three.

Dress to Impress

After showering and applying several layers of collagen stimulants to my skin, I opened my laptop and typed "www.meetup.com," the world's largest network of local social groups. Browsing the Denver options, I decided to join three.

First on the list? A speed-dating event at a trendy tapas bar downtown in three weeks. Twenty men in two hours seemed to stack some pretty good odds. Worst-case scenario, I figured it would be good for a few laughs.

The second was a social club for tall singles. *I'm tall. They're tall. We clearly have all the important things in common,* I determined. The description read that the group met for occasional happy hours around the Denver metro. It seemed chill and noncommittal, so I subscribed to receive updates.

Last was a young professionals' wine-tasting event. "*TONIGHT AT 7:00PM!*" the invitation flashed in deep Merlot red. I stared at the thirty-five-dollar ticket price, my finger hovering over the mouse.

Not only was thirty-five dollars more than I wanted to spend for a night with strangers; it would also wipe out my cherished fun money until June. After a sloppy April, I was back on track with my finances, health goals, and Bible reading plan. My ultra-tight budget allowed just one small luxury each month. I could use the thin cash envelope for life's simple pleasures. A new tube of mascara, a lunch date with friends, or . . .

Holding my breath, I clicked submit on the registration form. My luxury for May? The entrance fee for wine tasting. With strangers.

Within seconds, a pop-up appeared. It had the venue address and confirmation number, followed by three little words: "Dress to Impress!" My heart sank.

After dropping a size, I didn't have much to wear. In the old days, the solution would have been just to purchase new clothes. But with a ride-or-die mission of becoming debt free, it was the "old days" I was trying to move away from.

Instead of buying new things, I was subletting my apartment's spare bedroom for extra income. Using Craigslist and Marketplace to downsize, I continued simplifying at home. I kept a bare-bones, no-frills budget, purchasing everyday items using only cash.

Before the dating challenge started, I cobbled together one outfit to wear on every first date the entire six months. The idea came from my friend Kacie in Washington, who was working hard to revamp her dating life too.

The concept benefited me in two ways. First, creating a capsule first-date outfit eliminated decision fatigue during a competition packed with decisions. Second, it was a budget-friendly move: one simple outfit, rewearable, and complete from head to toe.

Mine was a black thick-strap silky tank with a soft greige three-quarter-length-sleeve cardigan, both from Target. Simple black flats. A new pair of jeans from Old Navy. A thin gold necklace and faux diamond stud earrings. It did the job just fine for regular dates. Yet there was little it did to impress.

The only other option was a soft wrap sweater in rich emerald tones. After spotting it in the glass storefront at a local boutique, I waited for it to go on sale, then cashed in my entire change jar to buy it midwinter. I'd worn it only twice, yet each time I received compliments.

It was all I had, and I hoped it would do.

Raise a Glass

"Fake it till you become it," I coached my reflection in the rearview mirror as my rusty clunker turned onto Pearl Street. A light spring rain tapped against the windshield, and I felt grateful for the cloud of firm-hold hair spray I'd swirled around my head before walking out the door.

Pulling up to the curb outside the chic brick venue, I stepped onto the sidewalk, handing the valet my keys. Through the large windows, twinkling lights hung from the rafters, illuminating a buzzing crowd, alive with conversation.

It's not too late to back out, my inner voices prompted.

But before I could leave, the tires on my clunker squealed and the valet zipped away with my car. Holding my purse above my head, I ran toward the live acoustics drifting through the front door.

Upon check-in, three girls rolled me down the line. One struck my name off her list, the second handed me my name tag, the third grabbed my elbow and yelled, "Have fun!" over the noise.

"So, what exactly . . ." I spun back around to the hostesses, hoping for more coaching. But the wall-to-wall crowd of single professionals had already engulfed them.

Tugging at my sweater, I let my gaze drift across the sea of faces. Everyone had one thing in common. They were all talking to *someone*.

I pushed my way through tight circles, bumping along warm bodies until reaching the nearest sommelier. Grabbing a wineglass, I devoured his attention as he talked about the clean, cherry-like fruit flavors. The hints of wood with a touch of bitter almonds. The good balance; the long, dry finish. Anything to avoid standing like a fool in the center of the crowd, alone.

Forget talking to men, I thought. My new goal was pure survival.

Just then, two tall, strapping bachelors approached the station. "Fake it till you become it," I breathed.

"What was that?" One of them bent his ear. His striking thick, trimmed beard and broad shoulders gave me an instant sweat mustache.

"Oh, yeah. Uh, great wine." Raising my glass, I narrowed my eyes, a flirting trick I learned from YouTube. According to Victoria, a British teen vlogger, flirtatious eye squinting was an exotic and mysterious move used by movie stars to give their eyes character. I sensed I appeared to be missing a contact lens, so I switched strategies.

"I'm Jen," I said. Clutching my wine in one hand, I extending the other, praying one of them would take it. Preferably in marriage, but a handshake would suffice too.

Dreamy-beard man shook it and replied, "I'm Christopher." It was clear he was hitting on me, with an obvious pickup line like that.

Before I divulged that I hoped our first son had his eyes, his friend inserted a pickup line of his own. "I'm Jonathan."

Not wanting to hurt Jonathan's feelings, I addressed them both with an overeager confident hair flip. "So, have either of you been to this Meetup group before?"

Instead of looking at me, their eyes wandered beyond my shoulders. Following their gaze, I spotted two blondes across the room. If "dress to impress" meant bronzed, low-cut, and bedazzled, those girls totally nailed it.

Looking down at my modest long-sleeved wrap sweater, I took a swig of Allegrini. Without response, Christopher and Jonathan brushed past me, eyes locked on their targets, moving toward the girls at the bar. Revenge seemed like the only appropriate response, so I shouldered my way over to a couple of reds.

"Would you like to sample the Cab or the Syrah this evening?" the next sommelier inquired.

"Yes, please," I mumbled, pushing two empty wineglasses across the counter. Glancing behind me, I watched Christopher and Jonathan clink glasses with the blondes, their twinkling smiles lighting up the room like a Crest Whitestrips convention.

It felt typical, being passed up for the petite, the sparkly, the Barre instructor calves. Was that why it felt lonelier to stand in a crowd than it did to be tucked away at home, completely alone? Just the thought of my worn gray couch cushions made me scan for the door. I had shown up, hadn't I? The venue points were mine. So, what was the point of sticking around?

Drumming my fingers on the thick wood bar counter, I was startled by a loud voice clearing behind me. "Er-hem!!!" Turning, I saw no one. But then I looked down.

Meet Brent: a five-foot-two, fifty-seven-year-old "young professional," sporting a stained Polo and pleated cargo pants. Note: I was pushing six feet in heels and standing in a dark corner with a glass in each hand.

Realizing this was no time to look desperate, I small talked with Brent for a few moments before abandoning half my drinks. Pushing through bodies, I shimmied through gaps in groups and clinking glasses. I had no destination, but I was on the move.

The room spun, shrinking smaller, as voices sparkling with laughter melted into unison. *I should go,* I thought. Turning, I scanned the room again for the exit. And as I did, my eyes locked with a tall, sandy-haired gentleman in front of me.

He raised his glass. Instinct told me to strike a power pose. And so I did. Quite unnaturally, I might add.

"Hi, Jen," he said. "I'm Kevin." Impressed by his confidence and his ability to read name tags, I shook his hand. We began a simple exchange: how we spent our free time, our mutual interest in writing, and the careers that had brought us to Colorado. And then *it* happened. With less effort than I'd anticipated came a *ding!* I had given Kevin enough information he could contact me if interested.

Later that night I stood in the misty rain waiting for the valet. Smiling, I sent Lisa a text. "I love the dating challenge."

Though it was a small win, I was happy to report that I couldn't wait to get back out there and try again.

Working It

The next afternoon, Sunday, I flew out on a work trip and was gone the entire week. Because my schedule was packed unusually tight, I didn't make it to a new venue, nor did I meet any single men, and I worked out just once.

Lisa, of course, took full advantage and met three new guys, tried two new venues, went on a date, and worked out twice. No need to pull out your calculator; she earned 215 points.

There was, however, one major perk to my hectic trip. Every night before bed, I would pull up Match and Christian Mingle and spend a disciplined thirty minutes exchanging quick, short messages with a handful of new guys.

By the time I landed back in Denver that Friday, I had five dates lined up for the following week.

Sushi Lessons

"Okay, Jen. Just follow my lead tonight," Tom said, taking my sushi menu and handing it to the waiter.

My week of five dates had flown by, followed by another packed with six more. Eleven men in two weeks was more dates than I'd scored in two years. Was it a lifestyle I could keep up with forever? Absolutely not. But the near-daily practice was helping. I was now on my third date with Tom.

On paper, Tom hadn't seemed like my kind of match. But after attending a chalk art festival on our first date, a light rail adventure downtown for our second, and now sushi lessons on our third, I was beginning to change my mind.

Tom was down to earth, a total ham, someone you die laughing with, a guy I really felt myself around. His five-eleven stocky build and animated facial expressions reminded me of Jack Black. (*The Holiday* version, not the *Nacho Libre* one).

We were trying a new, packed-out, cozy little sushi place in Wash Park, a popular neighborhood in Denver. I was new to sushi, and an overall unadventurous eater, so the thought of consuming raw fish felt slightly terrifying. But, determined to keep showing up (even if it was badly), I accepted his offer to give me an intro lesson.

All evening, Tom gently guided me through each roll, sticking to a beginner's selection. As we talked, conversation was both fun and casual.

Per our competition goals, I made sure to ditch the temptation to evaluate him and instead spend the time enjoying his company.

At the end of our date, Tom picked up the bill, turning down my offer to split. And when he said we should do this again sometime, I agreed.

"Sounds great!" he said. "I'll call you. We'll set something up."

Driving home, I felt like things were finally clicking. Maybe my luck was beginning to change.

Tall Singles

A week later, I received an exciting surprise. It was a private message from a mysterious guy named Mike in the Tall Singles Meetup group. "Hey, Jen! Saw your profile pic on the T.S. Meetup page. Any chance you'd like to get ice cream next Saturday?"

My eyes widened. I had never been sought out like that before. It seemed all my positivity and hard work was paying off. Glowing, I responded yes to his invitation.

Saturday rolled around, and once again I forfeited my first-date outfit in exchange for the soft emerald wrap sweater. Applying my favorite lip gloss, I touched up my hair with some loose curls, then clasped a delicate gold necklace around my neck.

Walking to my car, I breathed in the flowering cherry blossom trees, still dewy from an afternoon spring rain. Behind me, a blaze-orange sunset illuminated the still-snowcapped Rockies on the horizon; the May air was fresh and cool. Glancing in the rearview mirror, my heart felt at ease, and I felt pretty.

I arrived at the popular old-fashioned ice cream parlor right on schedule. Stepping under the candy-striped awning, I pulled open the door and a bell above the frame gave a little jingle.

Mike stood just inside the shop. At six foot six he was hard to miss. "You must be Jen," he said. Sporting a black nylon jacket and dark blue jeans, he was slender with green eyes and dusty blond hair that flipped up above his ears, giving him a boyish look for his late thirties.

Grabbing a spot in line, he asked my favorite ice cream flavors. "The chocolate caramel swirl looks really good," I said. "Mmm, so does the marshmallow mocha." With a long line in front of us, we chatted about our height advantage, agreeing tallness came in handy for previewing flavors.

He asked if I wanted to share a dish, which seemed like a pretty romantic gesture. When it was our turn, he pointed down into the glass case and ordered a double scoop of strawberry from the girl behind the counter. Then he paid and grabbed two plastic spoons.

We settled into the last open table on red vinyl seats. My long legs bumped up against his even longer ones. As the jukebox played, we shared our ice cream from the cup between us.

After chatting about what we enjoyed doing in our free time, Mike asked what TV shows I liked to watch. He shared that his favorites were ESPN and Game of Thrones. Since I hadn't seen much of either, I asked him to tell me more. But honestly, we didn't get that far.

At precisely eighteen minutes into our date, the last spoonful of ice cream was lifted out of the dish. I know this because it was also the moment Mike abruptly scraped back his vinyl chair and stood up from his seat, bringing our conversation to a screeching halt.

My gaze climbed up his long, lanky frame until I reached his eyes. They darted. My chest pounded as he cleared his throat. Fumbling for words, he stuttered, his face twisting. "Well, uh, it was nice to meet you." Then, as if he had been waiting a lifetime to get out of there, he bolted for the door.

Breath left me, fast and hard, like a nicked balloon racing through the air. My gut ached from the punch, as if his blow had been more than just words. I sat alone, heat flushing my cheeks.

The room spun. A booth of toothless kids with chocolate lips giggled, slurping up soggy cones. Moms and dads worked in tandem, grabbing napkins, snapping photos, commenting about bath time. Under small marble tables on either side of mine, starry-eyed duos played footsie. Cast winks. Held hands.

But I sat alone, holding an empty dish and two plastic spoons. Unwanted, unchosen, incredibly aware of how foolish I suddenly felt. Fighting back tears, I gathered our trash and glanced at my phone.

No new messages. I never heard from Kevin at the wine-tasting event. And it had been a week since I'd heard from sushi Tom. There was no text from Mike, apologizing for his abrupt departure, and in that moment, the silence of my phone was the loudest noise I'd ever heard.

Blindly, I stood, stumbling toward the trash can, then fought my way to the door. The bell jingled as I left. Jukebox oldies and laughter faded behind me as I pushed through the rain that had once again started to fall.

The blaze-orange sunset was long gone, leaving a damp chill in the air. I shivered, fumbling for my keys. Warm tears slipped down my cheeks, leaving silent trails on my neck, mixing with the cold mist, soaking the soft V of my sweater.

Turning the key, my car rattled to life. I glanced at my reflection in the rearview mirror; I no longer felt pretty. Instead, the floodgates opened and new beliefs crashed inside my soul.

You're too much, Jen.

You're simply not enough.

You're not pretty enough, not small enough. You're too serious, straitlaced, a complete and utter bore. Not charming, sparkly, or delightful. You're not sweet and petite. You're unwanted, Jen, unnoticed, discarded.

Headlights pierced through darkness as the windshield wipers swished side to side. With their rhythm, their beat, dark thoughts barreled at me, impaling my heart, one right after another. I had been totally and completely rejected, and all I had was my imagination to try to understand why.

Too much.

Not enough.

As the rain pelted harder, my wipers picked up speed. The ache inside me grew, following their lead.

I wept for what I wanted with all my heart. For the girl inside me doing her very best, teaching herself to be courageous when she would rather be with good friends or just stay home. I wept for the pain of having someone take one look at my heart, one look at my figure, then run full sprint for the door.

My past was not haunted by endless walkouts or point-blank rejections. Until now I had never given enough guys that chance. Instead, my heart suddenly felt cut open by a feeling as sharp as a scalpel and as deep as a sword.

Unchosen.

Just the whisper of it hardened like cement inside me, adding another tough layer to my heart. Layers that were becoming hard to peel off, hard to keep soft, to keep vulnerable. Layers that made it hard to try again.

I wept for the goodness inside me, giving the challenge my very best shot. I wept for the woman inside me who watched the lives of dear friends gathered around tables with their husbands, their children, in their homes, with success, wishing to be spending my evenings as they did, sudsing up shampoo mohawks to soft-skinned toddlers in the tub. Not sitting on a cold metal chair across the table from yet another stranger, exhausted after a long week of work, still standing in the lineup of single women, waiting . . . waiting . . . waiting . . .

When I opened the door to my apartment, it was dark, but I did not turn on the lights. Instead, I walked past the bathroom and down the hall to my bedroom, then shut the door and climbed into bed.

Burying myself in the comfort of the cool cotton sheets, I whispered, "I hate the dating challenge." And then I cried myself to sleep.

Chapter 7 | UnRejectable

"Hey baby, I noticed you noticing me; so, I just want to put you on notice that I noticed you too."

~ Fresh Prince of Bel-Air

"I can buy you another box of Kleenex," I said to my counselor. We were less than halfway through my second session, and already the trash can between our feet overflowed.

Thoughts of my date's dash had lingered with me over the next several days. I shared with her that the reality was my heartache wasn't just about Mike at the ice cream shop. Earlier that week, I went on a first date with a general contractor named Matt. The waitress had barely taken our breakfast orders when his true agenda was revealed.

"Tell me more about your sister," he'd said.

"My sister?" I asked, trying to connect the dots.

"Yeah, the one next to you in that profile picture at Red Rocks Amphitheatre." My mind flashed back to Lisa's visit in February. We snapped a sister selfie the day she flew out, and I'd used it for one of my online dating pictures.

After drilling for info about her, he asked if I'd mind setting him up. I called Lisa that afternoon to let her know she might be receiving a call from my date. Trying to shrug it off, I'd joked at least I got 25 points and a free omelet out of the deal.

But it was hard to shake the feeling that maybe if I were a little more like her and a little less like me, I might have better luck.

Then of course there was Tom, my sushi date. We went out three times, each one a total blast. But then I never heard from him again, and just like Mr. Strawberry Ice Cream, I had no idea why.

Ghosting is the gut-stabbing trend of twenty-first-century dating and what *Urban Dictionary* describes as "when a person cuts off all communication with their date with zero warning beforehand."

While I hadn't started us a wedding Pinterest board or anything, after three dates, it felt human to desire closure. We were just two people having fun. Then poof, just like that, he was gone.

Homework

After emptying the contents of my heart on the table, I paused to take a breath. My counselor closed her notebook and announced, "All right, you've got more homework this month."

Inching to the edge of my seat, my mind raced through all the self-care goodies she was undoubtedly about to give me . . .

One-month unlimited membership of baby goat yoga? Complimentary bath bombs? A soft cozy throw pillow? Gratis bag full of antioxidant-boosting skin care samples?

Cupping my hands in anticipation, I held them out, waiting for her to make it rain.

"I want you to keep getting rejected," she said bluntly. My hands dropped.

Staring at her, I wondered how I could be paying such a cruel and horrible person to help me with all my problems. *Keep getting rejected?!* I wanted to shout. For how long?

My heart begged for hard numbers, tangible facts, someone to tell me how many more battle wounds I needed to endure before the story had a different ending. If I knew there was hope, I could go another thirty rounds, maybe even fifty. But rejection for rejection's sake? I could think of better ways to spend my time.

As I drove home, my mind traveled back to my very first online date. I was twenty-nine years old and had just joined eHarmony. At the time it felt like being one step away from submitting my height, weight, and cooking abilities to a mail-order bride catalog.

On the way to meet the guy at a Joe's Crab Shack in St. Paul and in major need of a pep talk, I called my childhood friend Ann Marie. Tender and compassionate, she was a patient listener as I confessed every nerve. When I finally fell silent, she simply said, "Just don't forget to have fun, Jen."

I wasn't expecting that. Even now, years later, they were words I often remembered.

There were so many things in my life I considered fun, but it never crossed my mind that dating could be one of them. Risky, yes. Exhausting, for sure. Confusing, totally. Uncertain, always. But fun? Dental work and pore extractions all ranked higher on my list.

Yet wasn't that one of the reasons Lisa and I started a dating challenge in the first place? Wasn't it one of our greatest hopes that someway, some-how, dating could be fun?

But now, over three decades into life, I wondered if it was too late. I was simply losing interest in getting out there and trying again.

Inner Voices

"Excuse me, is someone sitting here?"

Glancing up from my laptop, I was surprised to see a single guy my age pointing at the deep leather chair next to mine. I had just finished a work meeting in Boulder and decided to knock out a few emails at Starbucks while traffic on Highway 93 simmered.

Without a word, I shook my head. He took a seat and began to set up shop; I could've cared less. After the *Matt, Mike, and Tom Show*, I decided I was better off hot-gluing my heart shut, pulling down the blinds, wrapping it with barbwire, installing a state-of-the-art alarm system, then setting it on fire, and moving into a convent. Some things just make sense, amiright?

We sat there typing away in silence, each pausing only occasionally to reach for our drinks on the small wooden table between us. I didn't have to glance at him to know he was an attractive guy. I'd seen it the moment he asked to sit down; I felt it as his presence warmed the space.

You should introduce yourself, an inner voice piped up. That surprised me. I swore those voices had gone down in flames with the rest of the contents of my heart.

I explained to the inner voices, as plainly as I could, that men wanted the Lisas of the world. Not the Jens. *And besides,* I continued, *what would I even say?* Without waiting for an answer, I stomped those voices deeper into the abysmal void where they belonged.

Within moments, they wriggled free. *Try again,* came a whisper, louder this time.

And say what? I rolled my eyes, reaching for my tea.

Just then, the heavens broke open, beaming a spotlight on a white envelope between our cups. A harmonic halleluiah chorus burst forth as I scanned the label. It was addressed to Pastor Kyle. Exhaling slowly, I knew what I needed to do. And I wasn't really feeling inspired to do it.

"So," I started, "you're a pastor?"

A questioning look spread across his face. "Yeah, youth pastor. How did you know?"

My eyes dropped to the envelope between us. "Lucky guess, I suppose."

He laughed. I stopped breathing.

I admit, I had already determined what the outcome would be if I chose to continue conversation, and it did not end with success. The guy was a pastor. It was basically his job to be nice to me. And he was definitely not interested. *Leave the rugged thirty-something alone, Jen,* the inner voices chided. *I repeat: step away from the single youth pastor.*

Conversation faded and we both turned back to our computers. Lingering self-doubts scored another point, bringing the new total to something like Self-Doubt = 563; Jen = ZERO. Yes, maybe I'd learned how to assert a conversation starter in April. But the confidence to believe I was charming enough to get the guy? Nothing but a pile of ice-cold coals left over from an abandoned fire.

The counselor's words flashed. *I want you to keep getting rejected, Jen.* My bruised heart ached for mercy, begged not to try again. Uncrossing my arms, I softened, inviting my body to relax.

"I'm Jen, by the way."

Kyle looked back up and smiled, "Nice to meet you, Jen."

I asked where he worked. He shared a community church nearby, then returned the serve. I asked what he enjoyed about his role; he volleyed back with a few questions of his own. After ten minutes of small talk, it emerged he had minored in Greek.

With an impulse that floored me, I asked, "So, um, do you give private Greek lessons?" My heart screamed in terror. *Private Greek lessons?!?!* What kind of question was that?

To my surprise, he pulled out a business card and said, "Sure, I gave a few tutoring sessions during my graduate studies."

I wasn't quite sure what to do next. So, I said the only thing that came to mind.

"Well, if you're ever in need of a free skin care consultation, here's my contact info too." He looked amused as he took my card.

Driving home, I reflected on those few moments that self-doubt cornered my soul and nearly won. I came so close to listening to those thoughts, and now that it was behind me, I didn't even care about the scoreboard. My greatest success went beyond 50 points.

The next day, I was driving home from work when my cell phone rang. It was a number I had never seen before. Thinking it was a client, I answered, "Hello, this is Jen."

"Hey, Jen. It's, um, Kyle. From the coffee shop."

I almost drove off the road.

He called to say he really enjoyed talking and would love to take me on a date that weekend. "That is, if you're okay with skipping the Greek lessons," he laughed.

As he spoke, a lifetime of scenes flashed before me. How many times could I have walked up, introduced, said hello, or gotten to know someone . . . but hadn't? How many stories of my life could have had a different ending if, instead of passively fading into the woodwork, I allowed myself to extend a handshake, a smile, or a hello?

Maybe great stories weren't about getting a number, a date, or an *I do*. Perhaps for a story to truly be great, it required only one thing: to be brave.

"I'd love to, Kyle."

As we set details, I realized rejection wasn't truth. It's just somebody's opinion.

Besides, I'm more of a chocolate ice cream kind of girl anyway.

Smarter vs. Harder

The moment I began pushing hard against my fear of rejection was the moment I discovered how Lisa had been so powerful all along. Why hadn't I seen it before? While I collected excuses the way a fourth-grade boy does baseball cards, she was constantly burning all of hers to the ground.

Over the following weeks, Lisa never once complained about living in a town so small you don't want to blink or you'll miss it. Instead of focusing on the hurdles of dating, she created opportunities.

May was high school graduation month. Because of her job with Young Life, she knew most kids in the county. Every weekend was packed with grad parties. And with each party came carloads of older male cousins, single uncles, and old family friends.

We agreed graduation parties counted as new venues. Technically, they fit our description: 1) a place she didn't ordinarily go; 2) surrounded by people she wasn't ordinarily with; 3) and going with the intention of meeting new single guys.

Despite our competitive smack talk, we always respected each other, asking for a stamp of approval when it came to points. Our game aimed to encourage each other toward becoming better versions of ourselves. If Lisa could use graduation parties to do that, more power to her.

It turned out to be an amazing strategy too. Who knew so many single men would pour into her rural Idahoan town that month? Twelve bachelor phone numbers later, Lisa remained in the lead.

By striking up convos and dishing out contact info for 50 points a pop, Lisa worked smarter, not harder. I, on the other hand, continued snagging dates through online sites for points. In the first three weeks of May, I went on fourteen of them.

Fourteen dates. IN THREE WEEKS.

I was barely alive.

Working twice as hard for half the points still seemed less intimidating than walking up to single men and hitting home run conversations. Sure, I had jumped the hurdle of rejection and lived to tell the tale. But I was learning that just because something was simple did not mean it was easy.

Graduation parties weren't the only place Lisa hit the jackpot. There was also Whiskey Jacques, a local venue with live music and dancing. Despite not drinking, she knew how to kick up her heels and have a good time. Four single men kept her spinning all night, then wouldn't let "a pretty gal like her" leave without exchanging numbers.

With only forty-eight hours left in May, I needed a rocket launcher of my own to blast me toward the finish line. Or at least a solid 400-plus points. As luck would have it, my speed-dating event was that night. And I was Bachelorette #9.

Speed Dating

The swanky downtown lounge was dimly lit, which I figured could work both for and against me. Low lighting was critical for muting an undesirable glistening brow in the presence of a dreamboat. Then again, it could also mask weird unattended-nose-hair situations in the evening's lineup of bachelors.

Cozying into a quaint half booth with red velvet seats and a small tealight candle, I peeled off the back of my name tag and pressed it on my cardigan. Opening my thick white speed-dating card, I scanned the twenty blank lines to write each gentleman's name. Next to each line were three boxes:

☐ YES ☐ NO ☐ MAYBE

Glancing around the room, I saw a few men in dress shirts and slacks making small talk at the bar. They carried white cards too. *What if every guy checks* no *by my name?* The thought didn't do me any favors.

A few girls my age gushed over each other at the front table, their outfits trendy, posh, modern, cute. *I knew I should have worn the emerald sweater,* I thought, dropping my eyes to my plain, pressed first-date outfit. But late May weather was too hot for that sweater. It was the basic black tank and lightweight greige cardigan from here on out.

My thoughts were interrupted by the distinct ring of a bell. Melanie, our platinum-blonde, sequin-bedazzled hostess grabbed a microphone. "Find your seats! We start in two minutes!"

Taking a deep breath, I released it slowly and tried to look important by staring at my phone. Within seconds, I heard, "Hello, senorita."

Pulling out the chair across from my little half booth, a gentleman with caramel skin and a bright white smile sat down. "My name is Santiago. And yours?"

"Jen." We penciled one another's names onto the first blank line, and I wondered if it was premature to dot the "i" in Santiago with a heart. I refrained.

Melanie swept toward the center of the room like she was auditioning as a Beyoncé backup dancer with something to prove. With both hands on the mic, she announced the evening's rules:

- Women remain seated the entire evening; men rotate tables.
- Every five minutes, a bell rings, signaling to rotate. At that point, check *yes, no,* or *maybe.*
- At the end of the night, write down whom you'd like to see again and turn the card into the hostess.
- The next day, you receive an email with your mutual matches.

Flashing a smile with more wattage than the Eiffel Tower, Melanie shouted, "Let the games begin!" Then, like a shotgun start at a track meet, she gave the bell a loud introductory ring, and the room of forty singles erupted into conversation.

My speed date with Santiago flew by. To be honest, I have no recollection what we talked about. There is a solid chance I just sat there, drinking in his dark-chocolate-brown eyes. By the time the bell rang, signaling men to rotate, I checked *maybe* next to Santiago's name.

For the next ninety-five minutes, I went on speed dates with nineteen more men.

My sixteenth speed date of the night looked like your average Joe . . . except his name was Nate. There was nothing special about the way he dressed: basic jeans, worn button-up. He didn't have the most creative questions of the night, yet for some reason I liked him best. Sometimes it's those people you least expect who spark something inside, moving you to want to know them more.

Exhausted, I turned my card into Melanie at the end of the night. Inside, I had checked *yes* next to seven bachelors. Like the high school SATs, the night left me with little idea of how I'd done. But I knew I'd given it all I had.

Tight Green Buds

The next morning, on the last day of May, I went to the gym and climbed onto my favorite elliptical in front of the large picture window. After queuing up my playlist, I tapped my email app, curious to see if I'd received my matches.

Sure enough, there on the screen was a new email with "Speed Dating Results!" keyed across the subject line. Only mutual matches would be revealed. Had any of my seven checked *yes* next to my name? I wondered.

Steadying myself on the machine, I watched the large tree outside my gym's second-story window sway in the breeze. Tight green buds were beginning to open, giving way to the life each one had inside. Its branches were softer than they'd been two months earlier. Bendable, flexible, less fragile in the wind.

Looking back down at my phone, I reminded myself rejection was a part of life. There was risk if I made a move, and there was risk if I stayed the same. The only question was, which kind of risk was I going to live by?

I clicked on the email and was instantly greeted by three little names, photos, and email addresses. And there, right at the top, was that average Joe named Nate.

I want you to keep getting rejected, the counselor had said. And now there I was, beginning to see how much life was on the other side of fear.

Chapter 8 | Learning to Speak Man

"It's like, yes, I wanna hear about your fantasy football team, of course! Don't leave anything out."

~ Amy Schumer, comedian

"Headed to Barnes & Noble to read *Sports Illustrated* this afternoon. Pray for me," I text-joked to Lisa.

It was the first day of June and the kickoff of our newest monthly theme, Learning to Speak Man. Our mission was to check off thirty "mantivities" in thirty days for 10 points each. Plus, a bonus 50 points for whoever completed them all.

Mantivities were what Lisa and I nicknamed stereotypical manly activities. Our list contained things like chopping wood, watching sports, playing video games, grilling out, test driving trucks, going to an all-you-can-eat buffet, and reading books that promised to reveal the secrets of a man's soul—just to name a few. Everything but *grow a beard* and *lasso a venomous snake* made the cut.

We had three goals for taking a deep dive into the cliché, because Lord knows women can do all those things too. Even grow a beard. (Reason #573 aestheticians, aka your local hair removal specialists, are a girl's best friend.)

The first goal was simple: to improve our conversations with guys. Two months in, we noticed certain topics sparked more intrigue on dates than others. Like the mention of our glory days, growing up fishing each summer with our family, or reminiscing about cheering for our cousin during his stint playing baseball in both the minor and major leagues.

These were small slices of common ground—quick connection points—with women who, respectively, worked with teens and gave facials for a living. Lisa and I were curious: could tackling a list of thirty mantivities help us connect even better with guys?

Our second goal was to have some straight-up, good old-fashioned adventurous fun. Lisa and I (along with Emily and our brother, Brian) were raised by a mom with four brothers and a dad who regularly schooled us like a troop leader does his Boy Scouts. Childhood was spent building rockets and forts, reading vintage *Hardy Boys*, and portaging canoes and Duluth Packs across the rugged Minnesota Boundary Waters.

There were never hobbies only for girls or only for boys—our parents raised us to know how to work a lawn mower or jigsaw just as well as an oven or washing machine. But that was childhood. Now that we were adulting, those adventures felt a million years old. We had a hunch the best way to have more fun with dating started with simply having more fun as singles.

Our last goal was to increase our odds of meeting single men by going places many guys spent their time. One thing Lisa and I loved about the mission of Young Life was its high priority on meeting kids on their turf. That meant cheering on the sidelines at football games and band concerts, volunteering in study halls, even hanging out at the smoker's pit. It was a way to say, "I'm interested" and "I care."

Many guys made statements on their online profiles sharing that they loved when a woman joins them for an activity. It was no secret Lisa and I hadn't met a single eligible while browsing nail polish aisles. But swinging over to electronics or hardware? Our odds of finding a man to strike up conversation with dramatically increased.

We had no idea if June's thirty mantivities would improve our dating game. It was an experiment, a hope. And we were ready to rumble.

Man-Mag Napping

Walking into Barnes & Noble, I wove through mazes of bookshelves to the large wall of magazines. It was divided into sections by topic and interest.

To my right, layers of glossy publications covered in bright pops of color danced before my eyes. Flirty captions like the "97 Ways to Be Superhot . . . Now!" and lifesavers like "132 Weeknight Dinner Solutions" begged me to roll up my sleeves and dive into hours of extensive research.

My eyes shifted left. Staring blankly, like a deer in headlights, I scanned the foreign wall of muted earth-toned magazines. Ironically, several covers featured actual deer in headlights. Also featured were camo, muscles, engines, guns, athletes, wood shops, and automobiles.

With a dramatic shoulder slump, I slunk over and pulled the latest issue of *Sports Illustrated* off the rack. Finding the nearest bench, I mentally prepped myself for 104 pages of industry statistics and beer ads.

I can do this, I thought, casting a longing side eye at the glossier color pops nearby. *Joanna Gaines, Oprah, Emma Stone, and Mindy Kaling will be right over there if I need them.* My dreams of trading in MLB stats for the latest *Vogue* were interrupted by a low, rugged voice.

"Anyone sitting here?"

Glancing up, I saw a guy my age holding a *Popular Mechanics* magazine. He nodded at the other end of the bench. I did a quick scan of his left hand. No ring.

"All yours," I said, racing through ways to keep our conversation going. After staring at him in silence for 43.7 seconds, I strung together my cool next line. "Soooooo, are you, like, from Wisconsin?"

As it turned out, yes. He was, like, totally from Wisconsin. Thank you, Green Bay Packers hat.

We chatted for a few minutes before diving into our manly reads (mostly because he stopped talking to me) but not before I gave him enough information to contact me if he was ever interested (which he wasn't).

Yet after two straight months of practicing the art of conversation, outcomes no longer mattered. It was becoming clear that the bigger wins were about flexing my bravery muscles, time and time again. Besides, 50 points was 50 points, whether I got the guy or not.

For the next two hours, I read every article, ad, and statistic from front to back in that issue of *Sports Illustrated*. Head nods were frequent. Occasional quiet snores were heard. A small amount of drooling ~~might have~~ happened. But I did it.

And no part of me could have ever imagined what would happen later that week . . .

Take Me Out to the Ball Game

Shawn and I were matched on a dating website. After tossing around several emails about our mutual love for camping and fondness for our Midwest roots, he asked if I'd be interested in tickets to a Rockies baseball game.

I loved attending sporting events and had a special place in my heart for baseball. In sixth grade I showed up every afternoon to our neighborhood field with a huge perm, bigger teal glasses, and a black baseball glove, begging the exclusive boys club to let me play. Weeks passed with no luck. Finally, I told the ringleader, the pitcher, that if he gave me one chance at bat, I would leave them alone for good. Eager to get rid of me, he obliged.

Stepping to the plate, I hoisted my hot pink leggings, snapping them into place like a solid pair of Spanx. The freckle-faced pitcher, tall for a sixth grader, stood sideways on the mound, smacking his strawberry Big League Chew. I picked up the bat, tapped it twice on home plate, then placed it behind my shoulder. The field of scrawny sandlot boys bent in anticipation, pounding their dusty gloves.

The pitch wound, then released. In slow motion, I swung my heart out, connecting bat to ball. The red-stitched white leather flew so high it got lost against the afternoon sun. As it sailed over the home run line, all seven fielders chased after it in one long Little League conga line. My large perm bounced in the breeze as I victory jogged the bases.

By the time the ball sailed back into the pitcher's glove, he turned to home plate and looked me square in the eye. The field fell silent. Then he shouted six words I'll never forget. "The girl . . . is on my team."

I said yes to the Rockies game with Shawn and considered it a double win. I'd be receiving 10 points for checking off a mantivity (attend a sporting event), plus another 25 points for the date. His invitation was truly the perfect package.

It was the ultimate summer night for baseball. Baseline seats, cool breeze, a stadium of fans totally digging the wave. Something about the warmth of that late afternoon sun and the crack of a bat dusted off old memories deep inside me. They took me back to that braver, fearless, pink-spandex-leggings version of me.

Shawn and I small talked and cheered through the first five innings. He was a big broad-shouldered farm kid from North Dakota, a teddy bear kind of guy. The date was clicking away, both smoothly and uneventfully, when all of a sudden, without me even trying . . .

It happened.

As Troy Tulowitzki stepped up to the plate, a mental snapshot of page 23 in *Sports Illustrated* hit my brain like a bolt of lightning. With my eyes steady on the plate and confidence strong as that sixth grade me with the bouncy perm, I announced, "Did you hear that with Tulo's .221 OPS, he's an early leader in the MVP discussion this year?"

Shawn's eyes left the field faster than a buttered bullet out of a pistol. "What did you just say?" A slow smile spread across his ruddy cheeks. In full disclosure, I felt as shocked as he looked.

With a quick mental snap of my hot pink leggings, I repeated the one and only sports fact my memory could retrieve after a two-hour man-mag nap. Shawn's broad shoulders shook as he chuckled.

"Wow," he muttered, turning back to the plate. Ten seconds later, he looked over and asked, "Want to have dinner on Wednesday?"

I couldn't believe the true words coming out of my mouth. "Bummer! I wish I could, but I'm going shooting at the gun range with a girlfriend that night."

Shawn's pupils exploded into pink hearts; fireworks blasted from his ears. "How about Saturday?" he asked, with a slight desperation I had never experienced from a man before.

"Saturday? Well, I actually have a tee time scheduled at the golf course that day," I said, pausing. "But maybe we could go together. You could give me some pointers?"

"It's a date," he grinned, shaking his head.

As the night went on, I didn't hide the fact it would be my first time at a gun range or that I hadn't hit a golf ball in nearly six years. My goal wasn't to trick him into thinking I was someone I was not, and Shawn didn't seem to mind. He said it didn't matter if I was good or not; he was just impressed I could let loose and have fun trying new things.

After saying good night, I got in my car and shot Lisa a text. "I can't believe I'm saying this . . . but the man-mag nap totally paid off."

New Promises

Before man month, dating felt dull, vanilla, basic. There was always a table wedged between two strangers, always the same metal chairs, same earthy jazz wafting through the speakers, same boring conversations . . .

"So, what do you do for work?"

"What things do you do in your free time?"

"Do you enjoy traveling?"

"How many siblings do you have?"

The whole thing felt more like a job interview than a date. Nobody likes job interviews, which is probably why nobody likes dates either.

Yet the longer Lisa and I tinkered around in man land, the cooler dating became. In our attempts to make the most of our limited time, we went double or nothing in the month of June. If a man asked us out for a cup of coffee, we suggested an activity off our list instead. That way, we'd get points for the date, plus points for the mantivity.

As weeks progressed, a crazy thing happened. Connections with men dove deeper than they ever had before. Even dates with total duds jumped from tolerable to enjoyable. We were talking less but laughing more. Lisa and I began to realize maybe creating a memory with someone meant more than words ever could.

I wasn't sure where man month was taking me, but I did know one thing: dating had never felt fun until now. So, I made myself a promise. For the rest of June, I would say yes to every opportunity to step out of my comfort zone that came my way.

Mantivities

"All right, let's recap our third week of Learning to Speak Man," I said to Lisa on Zoom, sitting up tall, my eyes twinkling.

"You're in a good mood today," Lisa said, taking a bite of grilled steak, hot off the grate. She was sitting on a bar stool at her kitchen counter, and I could see Captain Jack hopping around her patio behind the sliding glass door.

"Well, I've been working hard, Lis. You should be worried," I teased. My eyes moved to my image hanging in the upper left corner of the screen.

It was difficult to see how much I'd changed in ten months just by looking in my bathroom mirror each morning. But whenever we Zoomed, my reflection surprised me. I was not the same woman who'd answered Emily's Friday-night call the previous year.

That afternoon, my hair fell around my shoulders, a solid five inches longer than it was back then. A direct result of nutritious home-cooked meals and fewer haircuts while paying off debt. I'd also bartered with a hairstylist friend, giving her a facial in exchange for a rich caramel balayage.

I had joined kickball for man month and was wearing my gray team T-shirt with a pair of cheap aviator sunglasses on my head, ready for that night's game. My smile looked bigger too. Perhaps it was because my face had thinned, or maybe I had a few more reasons for optimism to shine.

As Lisa and I dug into our weekly recap, revival stirred within us, reawakening parts of our forgotten pasts. Learning to Speak Man gave us more than just a list of cliché places many men spent their time. Daily adventures were breathing fresh life into our nine-to-five souls.

That week, we'd experienced adrenaline spikes on winding mountain bike climbs. We'd taken trips to Best Buy to browse shiny gadgets and flirt with nerdy tech guys. On Sunday after church, Lisa had asked a leather-clad motorcyclist from her congregation for a spin through the countryside. And I had tried target shooting with a good friend after work, still sporting my black dress and pearls.

There was also Macho Movie Monday, the evening Lisa and I both watched a manly flick. To make the event as grizzly as possible, we each wrapped thick cuts of peppered bacon with more bacon, then slid them into the oven for a man-movie snack.

While Lisa queued up *The Godfather* in Idaho, I cranked up the volume on *Rocky* in Denver. Punchy theme music filled the air, while salty, savory, crunchy slices of bacon warmed blocked our hearts.

As the final credits rolled, tears poured down my face, washing away the bacon grease on my lips as I yelled out to my audience of none, "Aaa-driii-ennnne!" If there was hope for Rocky, then maybe there was hope for me too.

We read John Eldredge's book *Wild at Heart: Discovering the Secret to a Man's Soul*. I felt inspired when he shared it's important to do things that bring us back to the heart of God. The answer might look different for each person. Maybe it's a run, reading Scripture, silence, books, a sunrise, music, journaling, a sermon, or a wild and crazy endeavor.

A few pages later I grabbed my pen, jotting down a quote by Howard Thurman: "Don't ask yourself what the world needs. Ask yourself what makes you come alive, and go do that, because what the world needs is people who have come alive." A few pages later, Eldredge encourages readers to beat boredom with adventure. And just like that, it made a lot more sense why dating now felt fun.

In the spirit of man month, I uploaded a new photo to my dating profiles. In it a thick, scaly northern pike hung gingerly from my fingertips on a choppy gray Minnesota lake in a tipsy aluminum canoe. It wasn't the best shot of me, but it didn't seem to matter. Half the emails I got read, "Nice fish!"

Personally, I thought the photo was the least best part of my entire profile—no more electrifying than the part where I shared "Hair Color: Brown." In girl world, the picture of me at a work event showcasing freshly powdered skin and a great hair day was way cuter.

But guys didn't seem impressed by my street cred in the beauty industry or my list of favorite rom-coms. Yet that one slimy fish held high, right before I threw it back into the wild gray waves? That picture was pure gold.

Man gold.

I realized a catch like that could really take a girl places in her dating life.

Not only was June's checklist sparking more interest from men; it also provided more opportunities to meet them in our everyday lives. Like the morning Lisa asked her married friends Chris and Kira if they'd go golfing with her to help check a mantivity off her list.

Arriving for their tee time, they bumped into a single guy Chris knew who worked there. After introductions and some conversation, the guy ended up giving them free golfing. Not to mention Lisa earned 50 points for meeting someone new. The guy was a lot of fun and someone Lisa likely wouldn't have met without Learning to Speak Man.

Then there was the coed church kickball league I joined with my friend Jaye. Nagging fears like *what if I'm bad and everyone on the team hates me?* nearly stopped me from joining in the first place. After my tennis and softball careers wrapped up post high school, I hadn't considered myself the athletic type.

Yet I reminded myself our challenge wasn't just about dating. Lisa and I were going head-to-head with anything that made us uncomfortable.

Half the games I struck out with an embarrassing series of air kicks. On the occasion my foot connected with that big red ball, I rarely made it to first without getting pegged in the backside with it.

Even so, I kept showing up badly week after week. My hope? Maybe swallowing my fears in the small stuff would someday translate to swallowing my fears in the big stuff too. And the plus side, I was organically meeting teams of new people each game.

"So, are you ready to hear our new scores?" I smiled at Lisa, giving my eyebrows two flirty little pumps.

"Let's hear it."

Straightening my shoulders, I cleared my throat and announced, "For the first time in dating challenge history, I—the oldest and wisest and tallest and smartest sister of them all—am the proud owner of a 100-point lead."

Being the humble person I am, I high kicked and power posed and booyahed until Lisa finally interrupted with, "Congratulations on being the manliest."

After that, I stopped bragging so much.

As we wrapped up our Zoom session, there was magic in the air. We both felt it. Yes, Learning to Speak Man was a carefree theme, rooted in rediscovering joy, laughter, and fun.

But even more, our mantivities were having a powerful effect, both on us and the men we interacted with. Playfulness was inspiring confidence. Confidence was inspiring attraction. And attraction meant sparks were beginning to fly.

Chapter 9 | How My Feelings Are Feeling

Hans: *My lady?*
Anna: *This is awkward. Not that you're awkward. But just because we're . . .*
I'm awkward. You're gorgeous. Wait, what?

~ Disney's Frozen

"I had fun tonight," Shawn said, walking me to my car after live music, our third mantivity date. It was the fourth time he'd said it in two minutes, and he was taking just short of eternity to say good-bye. I knew what he was up to.

A man doesn't linger at your car door staring at your lips with eyelids as droopy as a basset hound's without hoping for a little good-night canoodle. He was still trying to formulate complete sentences while his lips were puckered in the shape of an O, and none of it was making any sense.

"I had a nice time too, Shawn," I said, stepping back.

I hated to be the killer of his dreams that night, but I was on a kick to keep the "grit" in "integrity." Kissing would break contract. It would complicate over three more months of dates with him and other guys. Lips were a distraction from the bigger picture.

More importantly, after three dates I wasn't so sure Shawn was my guy. On a surface level, there wasn't much attraction, though I knew that had the potential to grow. My hesitations went deeper than that.

Like most men I was meeting, we could share a meal or cup of coffee. A few hobbies, some stories, maybe even some laughs. Yet we did not share the one quality that mattered most to me in a partner.

My faith was more than just a religious category on my dating profile; it was a friendship, a connection, a submission to the God of humanity. My faith defined my values, my finances, my goals for the future, and the way I spent my free time.

It stirred my passion for teens and guided my quiet prayers throughout each day. It was a key reason I burned to become debt free, enabling me to give more abundantly to people in need. Faith was why I tithed 10 percent of my meager pretax income—a reminder to view God as my ultimate provider.

It was why I valued the countercultural message that sex was best designed for marriage. And why I loved books and podcasts from faith-centered leaders who encouraged me to live well in each of those areas too.

I was far from perfect in every possible way, often stumbling and in need of grace. But my relationship with God never felt like a bunch of rules; instead, it felt like a personal invitation to live lightly, unburdened, with purpose, and free.

When it came to dating, I wasn't intending to find a perfect guy. But opening my heart to a romantic relationship with someone? His faith values had to matter deeply too.

It was the reason things had not developed with speed dating's Average-Joe-Named-Nate. It was also the reason that, after getting to know him better, I couldn't see a future with Shawn, though I was glad to have given him a chance. Pastor Kyle and I shared similar values, but he was relocating out East, and communication had slowed.

"Well, I guess I should be go—" My words were interrupted by Shawn's face closing in on mine.

Panicked, I averted, then made the move every hopeful pucker dreads.

The side hug.

Unprepared to offer a simple explanation for how I felt, or the pace of dating I was looking for, I listened in horror as words tumbled out of my mouth.

"I was up all night thinking about you," I blurted. Shawn's eyes widened. *Wow, did that come out wrong or what?* I groaned. Then I tried again, though unsuccessfully, I might add.

"I mean, I've recently been thinking about how much I really, really like you. But how I just don't *like* you, you know? I mean I have a ton of fun with you, but my feelings just feel like maybe we could keep hanging out, but just as friends of course."

I tried to stop, but my mouth continued.

"Because I don't *like* you. Like that anyway." I paused. "Am I making any sense?"

Silence. My monologue even stopped the crickets' symphony dead in its tracks.

I'm not sure what happened after that. My subconscious burned and buried the memory of that painfully unprepared and awkward good-bye. All I know is I never heard from Shawn again and it made me sad.

When it came to becoming a kinder, braver version of myself, I wanted to do better, to be better. I wanted to learn to communicate in a way that respected and honored my fellow dates.

After three weeks immersed in Learning to Speak Man, I realized I was still fluent in only one language. And that was mine.

. . . And More Kissing

After I confessed my disastrous ending with Shawn to Lisa later that night, my spirits were revived listening to her own theatrical afternoon.

She, too, was noticing an increased interest from men during Learning to Speak Man. While at the lumberyard (for points), she struck up a conversation with a local bachelor. Impressed by her intrigue with sawdust and four-by-fours, he'd asked her on a date.

"How about a hike?" she'd responded. She knew she'd get points for a workout as well as points for the date. As an avid outdoorsman, he happily obliged.

They met at a heavily trafficked, short public trail. During their trek, his eyes widened, twinkling like glittery stars, as she regaled him with details of the ping-pong tournament she had played in (for mantivity points) several days prior.

The lumberyard bachelor couldn't resist. Right there on the trail, surrounded by a posse of kids, parents, senior citizens, and trail rangers, her date made a desperate attempt to plant one on her.

But before he could say "nunchucks," Lisa spun her twenty-ounce Nalgene water bottle like a pistol around her finger and shoved it right between his lips and hers. I like to picture their magnified eyes looking at each other through the foggy blue plastic, their lips smooshed onto it like a bug with a bad ending on a highway windshield.

No sooner had she lowered the water bottle, he looked at her with dopey puppy-dog eyes and said, "Aw c'mon, I just, er . . . want, uh . . . a little . . ."

Each stutter was another attempt to head-dive toward her, but he was no match for Lisa's catlike reflexes. After being Nalgened four times, he finally got the memo.

Her story gave me a good laugh on a day I needed it most. It made me thankful I wasn't out there doing this dating thing alone, like I had so many times before. Lisa and I were not just competitors. We were also there to cheer one another on.

And, for better or worse, we were there to push each other in ways we had never been pushed before. Which is how I found myself in an awkward position the very next day.

Baby Josh

Hey Jen!

I really enjoyed reading your profile. I would love to take you out this weekend! Let me know what would work best for you.

~ Josh

According to his online profile, Josh was in the third grade when I was graduating high school and making plans for college. When I received his email, I laughed. Out loud.

Hitting reply, my fingers hovered over the laptop keys. Without typing, I mentally played with my response.

Mmmkay, how do I say this?

I'm too old. You're too young.

Please, call me Ms. Carlson. You don't happen to have an older brother, do you? Or even a single uncle.

Isn't it past your bedtime? Wait—tell me that's not your headshot from your senior prom . . .

There was a lot I wanted to say to Baby Josh. I was in my thirties. He was fresh out of ~~diapers~~ college. My collagen was declining at a rapid rate, and it was only a matter of time before I discovered my first chin hair.

In fact, we'd probably both be getting our first whisker at the same time with that baby face of his. Sure, the kid had a nice smile, but who doesn't after a fresh set of braces? I just couldn't go through with it.

I typed, and I backspaced. I hit the keys again but with little luck at formulating a delicate response that wouldn't break his sweet little infant heart. Then again, I'd heard guys can have a difficult time with what we women refer to as "reading between the lines." Nothing I wrote seemed right.

Instead of crafting my rejection email, I called Lisa for advice.

"So, what do you think?" I asked after pouring through my dilemma.

"I think you should loosen up about your age difference," she responded. "It's not that big of a deal."

"Not that big of a deal?!" I shouted.

"Besides, didn't you tell me your goal was to get outside your comfort zone this month?" She pushed back.

"Ugh, fine." I groaned. "But if he takes me to Chuck E. Cheese, there will be consequences," I said grimly. "For all of us."

I might have thrown up a little bit in my mouth when I hit send on that email, telling Baby Josh that, yes, I was free on Saturday and to let me know where to meet him. Relief was mine when he responded with a local coffee shop address.

Mall arcade diverted.

He was quite eager in his response. I figured he had just received his weekly allowance and it was burning a hole in his pocket.

From Baby to Dreamboat

Saturday rolled around, and I dusted off my old Boyz II Men CD for some inspirational tunes as I made my way to the coffee shop. Pulling into a front-row parking space, I spotted a tanned and toned hunk behind the wheel of a sporty blue car in front of me. We made eye contact, and as we did, he waved.

This could not be him, I thought, returning the wave. *No way could this be him.* My list of excuses as to why Baby Josh and I would never work was instantly shredded as the Brad Pitt stunt double sauntered over, then opened my passenger door with his insanely beautiful biceps. He sat down in my car.

"Hey," he said. His crystal-blue eyes and bubblegum lips melted my heart into a puddle of pink confetti. He looked older than I expected. He was confident and broad, good looking in every way.

Extending his hand to shake mine, he introduced himself. "I'm Josh."

Under my breath I muttered something like "Okay fine, I'll marry you," but when he asked, "What was that?" I simply blushed.

"Hi Josh, I'm Jen."

His self-assurance transformed to dazed and confused; his handshake slowed. "Your name is Jen?" he asked.

My inner voices started bouncing off the walls of my heart: *Ohmygosh, no. Did I say Jen? Haaa! Nooooo, no, no. Well, okay, like some people call me Jen. But no, my name is . . . well, what do you want my name to be? Nbd, I can totally reprint the wedding invita—*

Dreamboat Josh disrupted my raging self-talk by reaching his golden-bronzed forearm up to his face to scratch his jaw. "Huh. I could have sworn your name was Anya."

I snuggled close as he pulled out his phone and scrolled through our text exchanges to see where he went wrong. The only problem?

"Um, Josh, sweetie. That's not my phone number."

The words were barely out of my mouth when another brunette pulled up and parked right next to us, looking at Josh, unsure.

"I'm guessing that's Anya," I said dryly, then leaned in, hoping for a good-bye kiss. Sure, it was against the rules, but it felt appropriate in the moment. Also: it was the least he could do.

Opening the door, Dreamboat Josh stood, then politely ducked his head back in the car and said, "It was nice to meet you, Jen." He then turned to meet his actual date, Anya, who appeared to have just stepped out of a J.Crew catalog and had the body of an elite D1 lacrosse goddess.

Confused, I sat like an idiot, watching my ex-lover explain to his babe-a-liscious hottie the mix-up outside my car window. Just when I thought the plotline could not get any worse, I got a text.

"Hey Jen! This is Josh. I've saved us a table inside!" I looked up at Josh outside. Then I looked down at the Josh on my phone.

Oh my, I thought. There were indeed two of them.

As luck, or unluck in my case, would have it, that Saturday night there were two single, blond, blue-eyed guys named Josh. Each meeting brunette blind dates. At the same time. At the same coffee shop.

Welcome to my dating life.

Trailing behind Dreamboat Josh and his new honey bear, Anya, I slugged into the coffee shop where I found my youngster eagerly awaiting my arrival. He had both the babyface and the poetic passion of a budding Leonardo DiCaprio in *Romeo + Juliet*.

But instead of feeling like his darling starlet, I couldn't shake the I-could-totally-be-his-babysitter vibe. Despite my feelings, I decided to make the best of it. For the next one hour, eighteen minutes, and twenty-seven seconds (but who's counting?), that little Leo was all mine.

I had no intention of leading the sweet cub along, but I did, when I sent a platonic text the next day that read "Thank you for the cup of coffee; it was nice to meet you, Josh."

I thought for sure my use of a period instead of an exclamation point, along with my lack of emojis, made it clear I was trying to gently close the door on our date, forever and ever and ever and ever.

But when my phone started blowing up with flirty unwanted texts back, like "Well, it was easy to buy a cup of coffee for such a strong and beautiful woman like you," followed by a wink, I realized I still had a long way to go when it came to Learning to Speak Man.

Be Kind. Be Clear. Be Positive. Be Brief.

Communicating with men was different than conversing with women, and I knew it was time I made a greater effort in learning the male language.

In less than three months, I'd been on nineteen dates plus messaged with dozens of other guys who never panned out. In each scenario, either the guy or I said, *You're just not the right fit, and I'm moving on.* Of course, that didn't always happen in plain English.

And modern dating had terms for it all.

There was ghosting, haunting, and bread-crumbing. Catch-and-release, flexing, and benching. There was cricketing, catfishing, cushioning, discarding. Gaslighting, love bombing, hoovering, and mosting. Orbiting, peacocking, roaching, serendipidating. Tuning. Sidebarring. And even Zombie-ing.

There were a zillion ways to reject or get rejected—and to lose heart in modern dating. And for me, radio silence seemed more impolite than most.

But I was discovering one thing I hated even more than being rejected, and that was to be the one doing the rejecting. I knew how much it bruised my ego to be ghosted or to be used to get Lisa's number. To give the absolute best of myself only to receive dead air from them.

I didn't like the thought of rejecting another soul who was just out there trying his best to find his person too. And so, in my attempts not to bruise men's egos, there I was, coding thank-you texts by stamping my sentences with either a period or an exclamation point, depending on if I liked the guy or not. And then wondering why they weren't getting my vibe.

"Thank you for the coffee."

"Thank you for the coffee!"

These meant two totally different things in my book. But men weren't speaking my language. They were speaking theirs.

During man month I'd read a couple of neuroscience articles about the differences between the male and female brain. The nerd in me found it fascinating how experts have been studying the variances between them in chemistry, structure, blood flow, and brain activity since the Greeks in 850 BC.

I learned women's brains, generally speaking, tend to ruminate on and revisit emotions more than the male brain. When it came to dating, it was no secret my thoughts constantly spun and tangled, running into each other, breathing down each other's necks, all up in each other's business.

My feelings were always wondering how my other feelings were feeling, and the whole thing made me feel exhausted.

In my attempts to go easy, to be tender, to do as little ego damage as possible, it turned out I was doing more. I wasn't communicating out of inner confidence; I was communicating out of fear. Fear I'd do damage, fear I'd come across flippant or uncaring, fear it was my responsibility to carry the feelings of every man.

Staring at the text from Josh, I asked myself, *What is a respectful, nonruminating, uncomplicated way to reject someone?* Four things came to mind. It seemed best to be kind, to be clear, to be positive, and to be brief.

Though my goal was to speak man, I realized those four simple words weren't only for guys. They were for women too. If it was my heart on the chopping block, I'd feel respected if a guy didn't leave me wondering or unsure.

I knew I couldn't change the way men closed the door on me, but I could change one person, and that was myself. Picking up the phone like the gentleman I now was . . .

"Hey, Josh, it's Jen. . . ."

Be kind. Be clear. Be positive. Be brief.

Communication Differences

Camped out in Idaho, Lisa continued meeting men on a professional level. There was the garage sale where she lingered long enough to meet two different bachelors for 50 points each. She attended a regional Young Life event and scored another 100 points. There was some brother-of-a-friend one day, and a firefighter the next. Every day, it seemed another eligible made her list.

Her wins made me think how communication hurdles go beyond just gender differences. I couldn't keep up with Lisa when it came to meeting new men. And she couldn't keep up with me when it came to first dates. Knowing who we were, it made perfect sense.

She was a social butterfly who didn't know a stranger, while I enjoyed engaging with one person or small intimate group at a time. And so, even more than Learning to Speak Man, we were learning to understand each other better too.

There were plenty of days Lisa and I drove each other to the edge of insanity. Like when she was off chasing rainbows and butterflies, and I was typing like mad to keep our whole coalition in working order.

I almost killed her more than once for forgetting our weekly Zoom calls. But she was just out there, being herself and enjoying the world. And I was doing what I did best, too, ensuring operations were running smoothly.

Being a completely different person than my sister was another reminder that relationships of every kind take a lot of work to succeed. Men and women were different indeed, but so are extroverts and introverts and coworkers and friends.

It helped to remember, everybody's got their own lingo, their own unique ways of thinking and doing, that required me to lean in, to take notes, to learn a new language. I still had a long way to go, but after a month of Learning to Speak man, it was a start.

Thank-You Gifts

"911. CALL ME!!!" I texted Lisa. It was how I began roughly 87 percent of my messages to her, ever since my first conversation starter with Neighbor McHottie on Day 21.

I'm not sure why, but after several months of "911. CALL ME!" texts, she had stopped responding. Something about a boy and a wolf, and I forget the rest.

Staring at my phone with laser-beam intensity, I summoned her call. Three hours later, my powers pulled through. After confirming that, no, I had not been kidnapped or fallen into a mineshaft, and, yes, of course I understood the definition of emergency, I shared with her the big news.

"I found a guy for you," I burst out, unable to hold back my excitement.

"Oh really?" she responded calmly. A little too calmly, if you ask me.

Ignoring her apathy, I explained I received an email on Match that morning from a guy named Will.

STATS: 32 years old. Math teacher + Young Life leader. 5'10".
Single.

The email contained flawless grammar, which, if you've ever online dated, you know is rare. There were no greetings of "heyyy" or "how r u" or "whutcha up 2," which were frequent messages from guys online. His message referenced several facts from my profile, which meant he was one of the few who took the time to actually read it.

Clicking through his photos, I noted that he had dark eyes and a goofball grin, was slightly balding, and had an average build. His "About Me" section was simple and upbeat and mentioned his faith was a really important part of his life.

"So, why don't you go out with him?" Lisa asked. I could sense she was unimpressed with my matchmaking services.

The thought had crossed my mind. However, I explained to her, there were two major problems. First, Will claimed he was five ten, which undeniably meant he was five eight in real life, at least two inches shorter than me. I had zero doubts about that.

Next, I reminded her about our upcoming sisters' trip to Glacier. After her plotting to set me up with the tall, witty Evan for four years, I wanted to see where that plotline took me. In only two months, our paths would finally intersect.

"Besides, Lis," I said, my voice softening, "I've been looking for a way to say thanks for gifting me my future husband." I said it as a joke but deep inside wanted it to be true. "What better ending to our stories could we ask for? You find my guy, and I find yours. Consider this Will fellow a thank-you gift from me to you."

I added that I'd go out with him first, of course, just to make sure he was a good fit for her.

"All right," she caved. "When I come to Denver in October for work meetings after our challenge is over, you can set me up with Will."

"Deal." I beamed. We laughed as I gushed over what a great story it was going to make someday, when she was dating Will and I was dating Evan.

After we hung up, I couldn't seem to wipe the silly smile off my face. The romantic and humorist inside me loved to imagine such an ironic ending coming true.

Chapter 10 | A Beautiful Way

Jerry Seinfeld: Again with the sweatpants?
George Costanza: What? I'm comfortable.
Jerry: You know the message you're sending out to the world with these sweatpants? You're telling the world, "I give up. I can't compete in normal society. I'm miserable, so I might as well be comfortable."

~ Seinfeld

Standing on the spongy black mats at my gym on the first day of July, a brawny, auburn-haired gentleman was pumping out more consecutive squats than I knew to be humanly possible.

Ten feet away I was also living my best life, doing what I did best: fake stretching in the corner while sporting my "It Took Me 30 Years to Look This Good" hoodie and a couple of morning-mascara raccoon eyes.

With a slow lean, I poked half my hidden face out from behind the racks of kettle bells to watch him like a one-eyed spy. None of this was doing a lick for my dating game. My prayer game, on the other hand, was strong to very strong. Heart bleeding in nonstop supplication, I offered up my routine request.

Dear Lord, may no man look at me, talk to me, or—for the love—smell me at the gym today. Ah-men.

Just then, Big Red strutted past my cobwebbed corner, where I busied myself with a sudden overeager burst of toe touches. He didn't cast so much as a glance in my direction. It was in that moment I realized two things.

The first was that, once again, my prayers had been answered. And the second? It might be time to get some new prayers.

Bending Stereotypes

With the heat of July came a new monthly theme: A Beautiful Way. A spinoff of man month. Only now, instead of earning 10 points for every cliché mantivity, we'd be getting 10 points for every stereotypically feminine one. And, of course, our usual 50 bonus points to whoever completed them all.

But how, exactly, could we define words like beauty or femininity? To be honest, they stirred up a variety of emotions for each of us. Like a crystal lake that's unclouded until your feet step deep; suddenly whatever is settled on the bottom begins swirling, making the waters murky and unclear.

We decided to start our research where all true wisdom begins: Urban Dictionary. One user defined femininity as "an approving word used to describe a sweet, inoffensive woman who wears fluffy pink sweaters and floral perfume. Usually, a passive bimbo with the intellect of a sheep. Sleeps with a cuddly stuffed bunny. The ideal that most men want and most women aspire to: not to be confused with feminist. Example: 'Surgically removed your brain? How very feminine of you.'"

While Lisa totally slept with a "cuddly stuffed bunny" (you did not hear it from me) and my favorite nail polish was definitely hot pink, neither of us wanted to become brainless, spineless bimbos. In fact, that was the exact opposite of what we were trying to achieve.

We agreed the word carried some baggage. Lisa, the mascara-and-Chapstick, no-nonsense sister, could change a car tire faster than most guys I knew. Though she loved her Sunday morning dresses and heels, she confessed the concept of femininity always tasted a little like weakness to her. She never wanted to be considered a ditzy, airheaded fluffball of a girl.

I, on the other hand, really enjoyed many cliché things associated with femininity; I'd even made a career out of it. But I had some genuine uncertainties too. The truth was, feminine beauty had always inspired some of my greatest passions yet also held one of my deepest wounds.

At eight years old, I learned there was a right size and a wrong size for girls. According to the unspoken rules of feminine beauty, I was not the right size. For starters, I was tall for a girl, and when lined up by height for school pictures or recess or lunch, I always stood toward the front of the line, primarily with boys, while all my small friends stood together in back.

That same year a petite girl in my class laughed at me and told me I was fat when we stripped down to our bathing suits at a pool party. It was the year I accepted that smaller was better. And just like hovering behind kettle bells at the gym, I began to shrink back. To try to fold and bend and compress myself into the size culture told me feminine beauty was to be.

Those cultural standards were confirmed year after year. Like eighth grade summer camp when I wore some cool hickory-striped denim shorts all the girls in my cabin loved. But when one tiny-waisted girl insisted on borrowing them, we all watched her pull them on, several sizes too big, before they dropped back down to the floor.

Thanks to another growth spurt, I had reached my pinnacle height of five ten while the rest of my small "feminine" girlfriends stood half a foot shorter. Sure, I was great at giving piggyback rides, but I was never the girl who could swap shoes or clothes.

For as long as I could remember, I had been all height and curves. And in those days, body positive role models were not given space on the cultural scene. When my brain was being formed as a teen, the trend was waif-like bodies, and they graced the pages of every magazine from *Seventeen* to *Vogue*. Flipping through glossy ads as a girl, I never saw a single model that looked like me.

Over and over again the message was clear: Not pretty enough. Not thin enough. Not small enough. Too tall. For many years, those messages stuck with me, no questions asked. When I finally began challenging them near the end of my twenties, I realized I had my work cut out for me. If your mind plays the same vinyl record on repeat for too long, it can become background noise you don't even know is there. It takes persistence to continue taking the needle off that spinning black wheel, replacing it with a new record—a truer, softer tune.

Lisa and I, we each carried some wounds, some hesitations, some uncertainties around feminine beauty. But we also didn't want to feel bound by the past. We believed that beyond our baggage and limiting beliefs, the power of femininity held some really life-giving gifts too.

Goals for a Beautiful Way

We determined our goal for July was not to unpack what feminine beauty meant to others, but instead to explore what it meant for ourselves.

Our mind-set would be centered around cultivating confidence, both inside and out. Releasing perfectionism along the way. Being courageous, openhearted, and unafraid. Tuned in to the needs of others. Comfortable in our own skin.

When I first moved to Denver, I was in a coed singles life group through my church. On a camping trip, we played a version of hot seat, going around the circle and speaking words of encouragement to the person on the spot.

When it was my turn, my friend Jesse said he would describe my personality as the place he wanted to wake up on Christmas morning. We all burst into laughter, because a) his girlfriend was sitting right next to him, and b) it wasn't exactly what he meant. After reworking his words, he explained my presence was hospitable, like a cozy home on a snowy Christmas day.

I never forgot that compliment; it was the best I'd ever received. But when it came to dating and meeting new men, I sometimes found myself hiding behind racks of uncertainty. I struggled to let that wonderful part of me shine.

Becoming hospitable in spirit were what Lisa and I hoped to explore in July. We planned to practice warmth and confidence, then provide a welcoming presence around guys—an invitation to men without having to smother them or beat down their door.

We would earn points for slowing down and enjoying some moments of wellness, like journaling, taking a bubble bath, picking fresh flowers, getting a mani or pedi.

Lisa and I also loved caring for others and wanted to become more intentional about it. So, we added things to our checklist:

- Visit a nursing home or elderly person.
- Write a handwritten card to someone who has touched our lives.
- Bake something and surprise a friend by delivering it to their door.

Like man month, we understood both genders could enjoy all those things too. Our dad was the kind of man to write a handwritten note to make someone's day, and he ran a nursing home, spoon-feeding residents on holidays when they were short-staffed.

I knew guys who got pedicures and plenty of great men who loved to cook and even bake. The month wasn't about polarization. It was, like every monthly theme, a way to hone in on personal development, as well as to make dating a little more fun.

Well, most of it would be fun. A few challenges were added to provoke bloodcurdling fear. While "wear bright red lipstick for an entire day" was totally my cup of tea, it made Lisa want to run for the door.

And while she loved to kick up her heels, for me to "go salsa danc-ing" felt like jumping out of an airplane without a parachute. Born with two left feet, I possessed the rhythm of a gymnasium full of fifth grade boys at a Sadie Hawkins dance. The only salsa I craved came with chips and guac.

Adding a handful of uncomfortable goals to our list was intentional. We wanted to explore the *why* behind our discomfort. Because ultimately, practicing confidence in all circumstances was what July was all about.

Two Left Feet

One week later, I stood pressed against a scuffed white wall in a knee-length black dress, nude nylons, two left feet, and, once again, Goji Berry red lips. Clasping my hands together in front of my waist, I looked around the room.

Salsa music was drifting through the worn speakers of an old Magnavox boom box that sat like a lone ranger on a TV tray in the middle of a make-shift dance floor. Speed-walking past it while clapping his hands like a tambourine above his head was our instructor, a man barely taller than my rib cage, wearing a tuxedo and sporting thick black oil-slicked hair.

Just then, a tumbleweed rolled by the dusty glass front door. I had flown all the way to New Mexico in order to keep my dancing skills anon-ymous. Yes, I was really that bad.

In reality, I was situated in Albuquerque on business for the week. The pre-dating-challenge version of me enjoyed wrapping up travel days tucked into my hotel room, ordering room service and watching HGTV. *Those were the days,* I thought.

My Latin dance instructor clapped his hands again, barking at all seven of us wallflowers in attendance to line up. Men on one side, women on the other.

There were three gentlemen and four women, including me. I was the only one under fifty—and without a mustache, for that matter. Because women outnumbered the men, my instructor paired with me. His forehead barely reached my armpit, which meant his face was situated right in front of, um . . . well, you get the picture.

To further spice up the experience, our makeshift dance floor was a DMV waiting room by day and a Latin-dancing paradise by night. As if I hadn't spent enough time in the Department of Motor Vehicles that past year.

Interrupting my thoughts, the instructor inserted a long, steady, high-pitched "Rrrrrrrrrrumba!" and began to move.

"Go left!" He reversed with a twist of his hips. My feet went right.

"Move those hips, ladies!" he commanded. Instinctually, I did the robot.

For ninety minutes (with a five-minute break for Double Stuf OREOs and Tang), I danced the rumba with Ricardo, followed by the salsa with Bob. Then the cha-cha with Dennis, ending with the mambo with Ron.

When the evening came to a close, I paused outside, staring at the wide Albuquerque night sky. A picturesque view of the twinkling Milky Way hung over three red neon letters, buzzing and flickering in the moonlight: DMV.

It was a fun night, a great night, in fact. To no one's surprise, I was terrible and so were the other dancers. Yet, as each man held my hand, attempting to take the lead, I couldn't help but feel like dancing was everything dating had ever been.

Men and women, asking to lead, asking to be led, bumbling around each other, one stepping left while the other steps right, just trying, hoping, to hit the same beat. I sensed each gentleman desperately wanting to be a competent lead, guiding our feet in tandem, in tango. Just as I yearned to be prompted and gracefully moved.

Yet the challenge we all faced, the challenge *I* faced was *how?* On the dance floor there were spoken rules. Specific steps, precise moves, a plan both partners adhered to. But in dating the dance between a guy and girl was much more vague.

As an oldest child, a goal setter, an independent career woman, I knew how to take charge. But with guys, I didn't want that role. I wanted a gentleman to spot me across the room, to walk over, and to start the conversation.

Turning the key to my rental car, I sighed. *Yeah right. Like that would ever happen.* The way I saw it, the chance of a single guy making the first move was as likely as a small child pinpointing the same star, night after night, in the brilliant New Mexico sky. What were the odds? Like one in two hundred billion.

Secrets to Spill

The next day, I sat at the Albuquerque airport, waiting to board my flight home. Crunching on a Thai coconut salad, I was catching up with Lisa, listening to her go on and on about some dude who spotted her in an airport the week prior.

"He walked up, sat down, and asked for my number!" she bragged. All right, Lisa never bragged. She just poured salt in my open wounds.

"I don't know how this stuff always happens to you," I said between bites of romaine. "You always have these random stories where guys come out of thin air and strike up conversation." I knew she had secrets to spill, and I wanted in on the magic.

"Okay, want to know what I do?" The suspense in her voice told me it was going to be something good. Something juicy, top secret, over-the-top good. She paused dramatically, then announced, "I just sit there."

I rolled my eyes. "*That* is your big fat amazing secret? You just *sit there*?!" My patience for her cute, spunky little life was wearing thin.

Using a life-coachy tone, she proceeded to give clear, step-by-step instructions for her "just sit there" approach.

"First, find a seat with other open seats next to you. Do not fill them with totes, purses, bags, or snacks. They must remain totally empty and accessible. Got that?" She paused, as if giving me a chance to write her tips down.

Instead, I took a drink of water. "Yes, your majesty. Go on."

"Okay," she said, thrilled to be back in the spotlight. "Next, you must hold no books, no phones, no laptop, no magazines, and no earbuds."

I glanced down. *Is she spying on me?* Piled high, both on and around me, were all the items she listed and more. Swallowing, I set down my fork.

She continued. "Lastly, scan the room for people to make eye contact with. I'm talking men, women, elderly, kids, everybody. When you do, flash a big inviting smile to anyone whose eyes meet yours. And that's when it happens," she said. "That's when guys approach me."

The whole thing sounded ridiculous, like an infomercial for the Flowbee or the Better Marriage Blanket. Just like those late-night infomercials promise to give a "refreshing vacuum haircut" or a "flatulence-absorbing blanket for two," I could not imagine that "just sit there" was the answer to my approachability problems. So, I did what any loving sister would do.

I decided to prove her wrong.

Just Sit There

After ending the call, I threw away my trash. I tossed my phone, laptop, book, and magazine into a tote and moved it to the ground. That left an open seat to my right. I refreshed my lip gloss, put in a stick of gum, and applied French lavender lotion to my hands.

Then I just sat there, smiling like a fool while scanning the general area. Within thirty seconds, a single guy nearby glanced up, his eyes catching mine.

Instinct told me to look away. I could hear that dusty vintage turntable spinning its familiar tune: *Not pretty enough, not thin enough, not small enough, too tall* . . .

There were many times in my life I'd let the record play out. But this, I determined, was not going to be one of them. Picking up the needle, I replaced that old vinyl with a new one: *Confident, worthy, fun loving, lovely just as I am* . . . I flashed him my most hospitable Christmas-morning smile. The kind where your lips widen, pushing up the apples of your cheeks, and your eyes sparkle, and the skin around them wrinkles just a little bit too.

Suddenly, the gentleman stood, picked up his bag, and walked over. He nodded at the open seat next to mine. "Anyone sitting here?"

Without bothering to pick my jaw up off the ground, I shook my head, and he sat down.

"My name is Joel," he said, offering his hand.

"I'm . . . um, Jen," I stuttered. In over three decades of existence, this had never happened to me. Ever.

In a world saturated with airbrushed images, curated social media, and a typecast for Hollywood's classic female love interest, it had been easy to grow up with the understanding that being a certain kind of beautiful was the secret to confidence.

For a long time, those were beliefs I just lived with, no questions asked. But as we sat and talked, I knew my skin had not magically gotten clearer, nor had my body shrunk any smaller. Only one thing had truly changed: I was getting faster at swapping out that record.

And every time I did, I saw how junky and untrue those old messages really were. There was a lot more to feminine beauty than what I'd grown up believing. There for the taking was freedom, confidence, and self-love.

As the gentleman and I said good-bye and I boarded my flight, I couldn't help but smile. Perhaps there was a little rhythm in my two left feet after all.

Big Red

The next morning, I rolled out of bed and stumbled to the kitchen like a drunk pirate, my sleep mask slumped like a patch over my right eye. I never was much of a morning person.

As I grabbed the refrigerator handle, my left eye landed on July's checklist, strategically taped to the freezer door. Partway down the list, my eye stopped.

"17. Get ready before going to the gym."

On the surface the task seemed vain and self-absorbed, as if Lisa and I couldn't bear to be seen without full-face contouring, lash lifts, and professional keratin treatments. But in reality we simply wanted to start showing up with our teeth brushed and without a hole in the inner thigh of our yoga pants. The struggle was real.

The longer we adulted, the more we could relate to what I called the "over-woman syndrome." Overworked, overtired, overwhelmed, and *over it*. Not really in a dramatic or hostile kind of way. It was more of a chronic sweatpants, dry shampoo, take-out food situation.

And so, we added "get ready before going to the gym" as a subtle reminder to practice showing up for life. The goal wasn't to go full-blown glam girl. Just a simple hygienic tune-up would do.

For 10 points, I replaced my typical raccoon eyes with a little translucent powder and dusting of blush. My sloppy side pony was transformed into a semidecent topknot. Breath was minty fresh, and my lips were a natural shade of Morning Rose pink. Flashing the bathroom mirror a quick power pose, I grabbed my water bottle and headed out the door.

I'll be honest. Walking up the gym staircase felt different that morning. *Wow! So, this is what matching socks feel like!* There was nothing toned or superhot girl about me, but there was one thing that I felt: prepared.

As my feet hit the top of the stairs, I saw him. Big Red. He stood, ripped and shredded and beefed, just a few feet away.

In the distance, I heard the faint sound of my inner voices whisper. *I bet he exclusively dates auburns with snowboards, nose rings, and cursive inner arm tattoos.* But they were quieter than before, like they were losing confidence every time I gained more of my own.

I flashed my very best full-wattage smile. "Hi! I think I've seen you around here before. I'm Jen."

The words sounded vaguely familiar as they rolled off my tongue, and I realized it was Conversation Starter #5 from month one. Only, this time it flowed like milk and honey and without the Tarzanesque vibe.

To my pleasant surprise, Big Red returned the serve and introduced himself too. We talked for a few minutes, and whether he was digging the conversation or just being nice, I didn't really care. I was reaching into the corner of my heart, spinning remixes like a late-night DJ, dropping the needle on fresh, healthy affirmations and thoughts.

Our definition of feminine beauty was not perfection. It was not about folding or molding or shrinking back. It was about feeling good in our own skin. Being less concerned with outcomes and more obsessed with living free. Everything I experienced at the airport and more.

Climbing onto my favorite elliptical that morning, I couldn't help but notice that the tall tree outside the second-story window was in full bloom, alive and electric in every shade of green. Taking out my phone, I snapped a picture of its branches stretched across the clear blue Denver sky.

For the next forty-five minutes I watched its leaves come alive in the breeze, waving right at me.

Chapter 11 | Cupid

"You are a beautiful, talented, brilliant, powerful musk ox."

~ *Leslie Knope,* Parks and Recreation

"Well, well, well. What do we have here?" I smiled, doing a double take as Lisa lit up my screen.

Her lips were poppin' in a cool shade of cherry red, set against her tanned freckled face. She wore a blue-and-white chevron-pattern silk blouse, and her long dark hair hung well below her shoulders, full of bouncy, fresh-cut layers. A big change from her typical thrift-store T-shirts, Carmex, and messy bun.

"Do you like it? It's an eighty-dollar haircut." There was a glimmer of mischief in her eyes; that girl was full of surprises.

"You little devil. I love it." Just then, her oven buzzer went off.

"One sec. Banana bread is done." When she stood, I saw her coffee table in the background. Instead of the usual playing cards and video game controllers, it was topped with several decorating magazines and a glass vase with soft white hydrangeas.

"Looks like you've been busy, Lis," I said to the empty screen, listening to her clang around the kitchen.

A minute later, she reappeared. "The lipstick feels pretty awkward," she admitted, but then quickly added it was good for her. Her personal goal was to feel just as confident wearing bold crimson as she felt belting out Disney lyrics into a big neon-green plastic mic. Which, let's be honest, happened quite a bit.

"So, I've got a date with Will on Monday. You know, the math teacher slash Young Life leader who is absolutely perfect for you?"

"Oh yeah?" She looked 97.4 percent less excited than I wanted her to be.

"I really think you guys are going to hit it off in October." I loved the thought of gifting him to Lisa. Looking through his profile, they seemed like a fantastic match.

Will's photos revealed they shared the same simple, no-nonsense style. His height was perfect; I guesstimated four inches taller than she was. He loved board games; Lisa collected them like it was her job. And, of course, there was the fact they both worked with teens in the same nonprofit. I mean, really, the whole Will-4-Lisa and Evan-4-Jen at the end of a dating competition? Every star was aligned.

After I finished filling her in, Lisa and I recapped our second week of July.

We agreed the month felt restful. Saturday afternoon manhunts were traded for bubble baths and much-deserved naps. Instead of hitting up the all-you-can-eat buffet, we earned points for doing random acts of kindness for strangers. Like buying gift cards at Starbucks, then peeking out from behind books to watch the barista pay our anonymous gifts forward.

The month felt communal, like when I earned points for #5: "Recruit or hire a style coach." Ashley and Sara, two fashionistas in my women's life group, volunteered to pile onto my white duvet one Saturday afternoon while I showcased my meager wardrobe.

Clothes fit me differently than they had the previous summer. I felt uncertain how to dress for those changes now that my figure had more curves. I also didn't have much of a wardrobe selection to choose from. But by the time they left, I scored fresh tips on maximizing my limited selection and complementing my hourglass shape.

Another night, my friend Anna and her mother-in-law, Kim, came over to help check off #2: "Have a spa night." We did DIY manis and facials, ate salted dark chocolate, then watched a chick flick. Not only did I score points for everything but the chocolate, it was good for my soul to invite other women into the dating challenge. Independent to a fault, I needed the reminder singleness didn't have to be done alone.

In the spirit of our monthly theme, I looked up the dictionary.com definition of beauty. I loved what I found. *Beauty*, it said, is the "quality present in a thing or person that gives intense pleasure or deep satisfaction to the mind." There were three examples:

1. arising from sensory manifestations (shapes, colors, sounds, etc.)
2. a meaningful design or pattern
3. a personality in which high spiritual qualities are manifest

As it stood, beauty was not thigh gaps or the absence of fine lines. It was not bound by guidelines and rules. It was an essence, a feeling, a sensory experience. Beauty was spiritual in a deep, untethered, and personal way.

It could be cultivated and nurtured into fruition, like a small seed planted in rich soil, given beams of sun, drops of water, and a gardener with the patience to watch it grow.

Friendlationship

As I shifted my beat-up clunker into park, it shuddered to a stop. I stepped onto the streets of charming old town Littleton, Colorado, and breathed in the warm summer air. *Tonight's the night!* I was beyond excited about my side hustle of scoping out Lisa's perfect match.

Inside the door of the small brick café, Will stood at (insert air quotes) five feet ten inches tall. Though he seemed to be fairly eye level with me, I determined he was either standing on a small slope or wearing lifts. Either way, I was certain he was shorter than I was, which clinched it. He was perfect for Lisa.

Our eyes met, and his face brightened. He let out a deep baritone boom. "Hey, Jen, great to finally meet you!"

I liked his enthusiasm. It reminded me of the Minnesota-nice culture I grew up with back home. Nobody knows a stranger; everybody's a friend.

We settled into a table for four, with plenty of room for my long legs and his big voice. His frame was average build, and he wore a plain black T-shirt that had a slight V paired with faded blue jeans, trendy frames, a dated watch, and worn brown leather shoes.

He was a math nerd, but not in a socially awkward way. He was confident, definitely not shy; the waitstaff loved him. I determined that he, like Lisa, had scored high in "WOO." It stood for Winning Others Over from Gallup's strengths assessment in their book *StrengthsFinder 2.0.*

I was in a fantastic mood, cheerful, upbeat. And I was "in it to win it" on Lisa's behalf.

"So, Will." I reclined in my chair. Power posing had always taken a lot of thought and effort on my part, but not tonight. Probably because it wasn't a real date, but more like a friendlationship starting to bloom. "Sounds like you love working with teens. My sister, Lisa, does too!"

His face brightened. I could tell kids were a real passion of his. But instead of asking about her, he asked about me. After all, my profile mentioned I enjoyed mentoring them too.

For the next hour or so, we swapped stories. Like the summer I brought my high school Young Life girls to the city park with a trunk full of ten-pound ice blocks at midnight. When it's hot enough, you can sit on them like toboggans, picking up speed down a hill.

Or the time he dressed up in costume and stood on his desk the entire day to teach. I guess anything goes when you're trying to rally high schoolers to absorb precalc and trig.

By the time our bill came, I realized I had run out of time to put in a good word for Lisa. He insisted on paying, which was very kind. We went outside and started walking to our cars.

"Pardon me," he said, taking a big step around to my left side. I wondered if his hearing wasn't so hot in one ear. "Sorry, I just didn't want to let a lady walk on the sidewalk nearest the street."

It was the move of a gentleman, and to be honest, I had never seen it done before. We walked and talked, and then before parting ways, he became a bit flustered.

"So, um, I'm not sure how this online thing works. All I know is how to be honest. And I'm thinking that if we both had fun tonight, we should try this again. No pressure, just two people hanging out."

I did have a lot of fun. So, I agreed to meet up with Will again, you know, for investigatory purposes. Plus, it would give me the chance to dive deeper into my matchmaker role.

"Sounds great, Will." We stood there for a moment, unsure what to do next. I offered a quick side hug; then we parted ways to our cars.

"I'll call you!" Will turned, walking backward across the cobblestone street. He tripped and nearly fell, recovering just short of a total wipeout.

Lisa's going to love this guy, I thought, giving him a little wave.

The Gentleman

Will did call. Two evenings later, just to check in.

He was leaving town for a couple of weeks, headed to a Young Life camp in northern Arizona with a group of high school students as their leader. He'd be returning late July, just when I would be leaving for a week-long work trip.

Our second meetup would have to wait until August.

"How was your day, Will?" I asked. As a teacher with the summer off, I figured it involved the snooze button and a pool party or a happy hour on some rooftop.

But instead of sleeping in and eating Eggo waffles or binging Netflix all day, Will shared he'd gotten an early start, mowing his grandma's lawn. Apparently, it was something he did every week during his summers off.

On his way home, he noticed a family with a flat tire on the side of the road. He stopped to give them a hand. Then he took his weekly coupons to the grocery store to stock up on essentials.

Will was humble as he recapped helping his grandma and the family with their tire. But he puffed up mentioning the coupons. I loved it. While pounding away at my debt, I'd become a coupon nerd too.

"What about you? How were your last couple of days, Jen?" There was a genuine interest in his voice, and for a minute I forgot my goal as matchmaker.

Will was a great listener as I took him, play by play, through my days.

After work on Tuesday, I knocked on my neighbor Nancy's front door. She was sitting with her eighty-nine-year-old BFF, MaryJo, at her antique dining table.

Hugging a paper sack overflowing with groceries, I announced, "Put your teeth in, ladies, and pull out your Bingo boards, because I'm cooking dinner tonight!" They whooped, then cheered. "See you in an hour!" I winked, before zipping upstairs to work on our meal.

The next morning I strolled through a garden center for half an hour, then delivered fresh flowers to a friend who had a rough week. After work I baked cookies to welcome some new apartment neighbors who just moved in.

I could tell Will was impressed, though my intention wasn't to impress. The goal was completing challenges from my checklist. My mission was accomplished and then some. The points were great, yet the joy I felt after serving others was even better.

"But enough about me," I said, playing Cupid. "My incredible, beautiful, generous sister Lisa had an amazing week as well." I could sense the weird subject change threw him for a loop. I shared her highlight reel anyway.

Lisa had called a stay-at-home mom with a wild tribe of energetic fireballs (otherwise known as toddlers) and announced, "I made a fresh loaf of chocolate chip banana bread, and Lisa's Special Delivery Service is on its way right now!"

When she arrived at the door, she offered the mom a much-needed break, then proceeded to check off "play with a friend's kids" from our list. She painted elderly women's nails at the nursing home one morning, then took a yoga class that afternoon.

By the time Will and I wrapped up our call, I felt satisfied with the good word I had put in for my sister. After hanging up the phone, I texted Lisa.

"Just had a great chat with Will. I think you're really going to like him!" I ended the message with a heart-eyed emoji. Then three more, because I'm extra like that.

That night I couldn't help but reflect on our conversation. I really admired the ways Will served others with his time. And I was pleasantly surprised by my own evolution too.

If a guy had asked me "How was your week?" before driving probation, I would have sputtered out a very different answer. One less focused on adventures and venues and beauty and others, and instead more centered around survival and myself.

Yet I hardly remembered her now, that old version of me. Making room for change played its own role in that, but it was July's rhythmic rituals of loving on others and self that were refining me, smoothing rough edges, like a gentle stream washing over pebbles and stones.

Will seemed to be responding to this renewed me. The laid-back, fun, kind and caring, confident-in-my-skin version of me. *Not that I care what Will thinks, of course.* I pushed thoughts of him aside.

Because: Evan.

Virtual Heartthrob

Later that night, at half past midnight, I lay on my couch, twirling my fingers around strands of hair. *I wonder if Evan has an online dating profile?* In my late-night delusion, it only made sense to take my research of him up a notch. I figured the more information I knew about the inner workings of his heart and soul, the better my chances would be of winning him over in September.

Instinct told me this was a fantastic idea, and yet it was also telling me to eat chips and salsa at 12:37 a.m. on a worknight. As it would turn out, my instincts were not the most trustworthy part of me.

Logging into Match.com, I expanded my geographical search to his city. I just happened to narrow the criteria based on what I already knew. And then, to my amazement, his profile just happened to appear. And the little green circle by his photo showed that he was online too.

Tall, successful, witty, faith-centered family man.

Evan.

Pulling my laptop closer, I cast a suspicious glance over my left shoulder, followed by my right. My roommate was dead asleep, but when people say stuff like, "If these walls could talk," even the Benjamin Moore Cloud White starts to look like a mole.

With a deep breath, I made my final click. Within seconds, regret washed over me. In all the excitement, I made two fatal mistakes.

The first was forgetting to turn on the incognito button. That meant when I viewed his profile, my face trumpeted down from the top of the screen with a flashing neon alert: "COLORADOJEN has viewed your profile!" I wasn't certain, but I think it also may have screamed: "Run, man, run!"

My second mistake was believing that reading his profile would put my anxious thoughts at ease. I figured if I could just read his description of the type of woman he was looking for, I could be certain I was everything he wanted.

But as I read words like *athletic,* then *toned*, my heart sank like a rock.

I could see the faint reflection of my cushiony curves on the glowing screen next to his photo. His big shoulders and side smile stared back at me, the image of a man who had all the boxes on my list checked. For four years I'd heard we were perfect for each other. So, we *were* perfect for each other . . . right?

I didn't say it out loud, never whispered the words *Am I enough? Am I too much?* Some part of me figured if I buried them down deep enough, my lingering self-doubt would just go away on its own.

But that's not how the laws of nature work. Whatever a person sows, at some point it begins to grow.

Anxious

Glancing at my watch, I bounced my knee impatiently in front of a blank screen. It was 4:09 p.m. Lisa was late . . . again.

Coming, Lis? I texted.

Per our "7 Habits of Highly Effective Daters Who Don't Get Killed" virtual blood pact, we committed to short recap calls each Sunday. The goal was to stay motivated and accountable. Update the scoreboard. Encourage each other. And, of course, talk a little smack.

The only problem? Lisa had a habit of forgetting our calls. She always apologized, of course, still breathless and smiling from whatever outing she'd come from. "I swear it won't happen again," she'd say. Until one week later, when it would happen again.

Staring at my silent phone—4:14 p.m.—I rubbed my face. A twinge of loneliness hung in the air as I glanced over my points for the week. In addition to some workouts and a few Beautiful Way activities, I had two first dates. Both were rough.

The first guy was from Christian Mingle and made cringeworthy comments not worth repeating. My naïveté took a moment to catch what his fetishes alluded to, but when I finally came around, I was too sheepish to speak up. Though the date didn't last long, I left disturbed.

The next guy was no better. Arriving in maximum sloppy form, his beer spilled on the table and ran down his arm as he swung it wide, railing the world. Brimming with toxic pessimism, he spent an hour unloading a lifetime of grievances and conspiracies. I am being generous when I say he possessed few manners and no social awareness. After that hour, I paid for my coffee, leaving absolutely drained.

When it came to dating, I wanted to remain optimistic and open-hearted. And so, just like my uncertainties after reading Evan's profile, I swept the discomforts of those bad dates under the rug. In each situation, I pushed away icky feelings, determined to keep showing up encouraging and kind.

My computer clock read 4:23 p.m. Still no word from Lisa.

Swinging the cursor to the URL bar while I waited, I logged in to Christian Mingle. Earlier that morning I'd sent an upbeat response to a new guy's message. "You love learning about finance? Me too!" I shared Financial Peace University was changing my life. Then I congratulated him on his recent move, warmly welcoming him to Denver. *Maybe he's written back.*

The little mail icon bounced. Sure enough, he had responded. But as I scanned his words, my heart dropped. He wrote back, all right: a six-paragraph blast over the stupidity of FPU and the idiots who believed its crap. His rant was fast and furious, like a bull who'd just seen red. There was little punctuation to his punches, as if he couldn't even come up for air.

His last line read, "So, wanna grab a drink sometime?"

I read his words once in shock. Then I read them a second time, heat flushing my cheeks. It wasn't that we had different beliefs about financial freedom. It was that he was mean, like a bully who never grew up.

I was still staring at the screen when my phone dinged with a text from Lisa. "Totally forgot about our call! Just wrapping up a bike ride with friends. Zoom in twenty?" It was 4:32 p.m.

My head was starting to ache. "Sure," I typed, then tossed my phone on the desk. I didn't have to say anything more. In twenty minutes my face would say it all.

Chapter 12 | Clouded Decisions

"If you ever start to feel too good about yourself,
they have this thing called the internet."

~ *Tina Fey*

One week passed. It was now the third Sunday in July, and I was sitting at my computer, eager to process another tough round of dates with Lisa.

She was leaving in a week to work for one month at a remote Young Life camp in Oregon. It was the same camp where I'd been a yearlong intern in my midtwenties. Eight years later, I still knew many of the property staff. I couldn't help but wish it were me, living the dream for a month, drinking chai in the plum orchard, reuniting with good friends.

The property was unlike anyplace I'd ever known, with a thousand-person-capacity dining room, complete with fine linens, a waitstaff, preset tables of dinnerware, family style meals, bottomless desserts. The ranch hummed with life and waterslides and well-manicured lawns.

There were climbing walls, race car tracks, zip lines. Volunteer adult leaders loving on teens, launching each other off the blob. Campfires under twinkling stars, dunk tanks, pies in the face, and kids and adults belting out lyrics to "Brown Eyed Girl."

Lisa wouldn't have cell phone service or Zoom access in August, but our game would go on. There would be plenty of handsome young adult leaders her age, being bussed in and out every week with the arrival of new kids. Believe me, she'd be just fine.

Pushing back a pang of loneliness, I tried not to think how in just ten days, I'd be doing the dating challenges alone.

Speaking of Lis, where is that girl? I glanced at my phone. It was nearly thirty minutes past our meetup time. I shot her a text to check in.

Within seconds, my phone buzzed. But it wasn't Lisa. It was Nathan, a new tall businessman with piercing blue eyes whom I'd started chatting with. My cheeks blushed as I read his words. It was a simple first date invitation, yet the way he spoke was bold and commanding, alluring, enticing. We had never gone out before. And something inside me tugged, warning me we never should.

Dropping my eyes to my watch, I shook my head in frustration. Forty minutes had passed. Suddenly, my phone dinged with Lisa's response. "Hey, I'm in the middle of some work stuff and lost track of time. Maybe tonight?"

Anger flushed my face and my body tightened. I'd cleared my afternoon for our call and had even confirmed with her the night before. Dropping my phone on the desk, I seethed. No response I could have conjured would have gone over well.

Tension had been thickening between us for a couple of weeks. She was becoming flippant, unapologetic when it came to missing planned calls. And my fuse had become short and atomic. It wasn't right for her to promise she'd be there, only to get swept up by something else and forget.

Though my frustration was justified, even I was surprised by how explosive and irrational my responses had become. Each blowup after a missed call ended with both of us quiet and somber on the line, asking if the dating challenge was worth our sisterhood, our friendship.

Sitting there alone, staring at a blank screen and silent phone felt like a Brillo pad being raked across sunburned skin. The truth was, my heart was already feeling raw.

In the past week two new dates had stood me up. The first time, I sat at the coffee shop after work, my blue jeans freshly washed and hair softly curled. Staring at the empty chair across from me, I texted him, then periodically checked my phone, hoping he was okay.

After thirty minutes, I tossed my tea and drove back across town in rush-hour traffic alone. He never did text back. Instead, he emailed me the next day: "I changed my mind about wanting to meet. Sorry, forgot to tell you."

My heart sank. *Maybe tomorrow night will be different*, I hoped.

But the next night was not different. Another man no-showed our date as I sat waiting for him on a cold metal chair at a café after a long day of work. Twelve minutes in, my phone dinged: "Too many pans in the fire with women. Not gonna make it."

Once again, my heart took a hit as I drove my rattling hunk of metal back across town toward home.

I had come so far in our competition, had felt the sweetness of our July checklist injecting life into my soul. I was working so hard to remain openhearted. But after reading Evan's description of his dream girl, followed by a handful of bad-mannered guys, I was feeling both defeated and tired.

Tired of deadbeat dates, tired of being just another pan in the fire. Tired of giving the dating challenge my all, then being met by empty chairs . . . at coffee shops, on Zoom, in cafés. I felt marooned when Lisa jumped ship, leaving me to weather storms alone. And I was tired of giving care sessions to bullies and slugs, or being overlooked by guys for the prettier and more polished.

I didn't want to throw in the towel. I suppose I just wanted to feel . . . wanted. Was it such a crime to want to feel lovely and date worthy and desired?

Picking up my phone, I opened Nathan's text, rereading the businessman's words. Bold, commanding, alluring, enticing.

My fingers lingered above the screen.

It was just one date. One dinner, 25 points. Harmless, really. First dates were part of our challenge, a new norm in my weekly routine. At least, that's the partial truth I told myself.

And so, it was in that clouded state of mind that I sent a text I would later regret.

"Yes, I'm free, Nathan," it read. "See you Friday at seven."

Unclear

I dressed in all black that Friday night: knee-length pencil skirt, silky V-neck short-sleeved top, a thick black belt clasped around my waist. Black heels, glittery jewelry, hot pepper red lipstick, long, loose waves pinned back on one side.

I turned side to side in front of my floor-length mirror. I was not athletic nor toned—but I felt elegant, channeling my inner Ashley Graham with her body positive, plus-sized curves.

I'm not the selfie type, but before heading out the door, I sent one to Lisa.

"Wow, Jen! You look fantastic. Hot date tonight?"

Reading her words, I felt a tug deep down once again. I shrugged it off. "Just another first date," I said, telling both her and myself the same half-truth. Per our competition rules, I texted her the address I was going to; we always told someone where we'd be.

Validation

When I arrived at the restaurant to meet Nathan, I wowed him, which was, deep down, what I wanted. In front of him stood a woman craving validation, which was, deep down, exactly what he wanted. Neither of us would have confessed our truths out loud, but we were just the kind of medication the other was looking for.

For every other date, I dressed like the girl next door. Blue jeans, casual silky black tank, simple flats, greige cardigan, buttons and all. But that night, I knew in my heart I was playing with fire.

Nathan's piercing blue eyes wandered all over me that evening, leaving no room to question what his intentions were. From his very first text, I knew better than to respond to a guy like him.

Words laced with seduction dripped from his lips, like the syrupy juice from a ripe forbidden fruit, each one more forward, more provocative than the last. They swirled in the air that thickened between us, and I was paralyzed, hypnotized, mesmerized by it all.

With cheeks flushed warm and crimson pink, I made a few weak attempts to guide our conversation back to wholesome material. He, in turn, steered things back to his menu of unrated commentary, in all fifty shades of gray, like an unstoppable freight train on a one-way steel track.

He cared nothing about my interests, my hobbies, my family, my job, that much I knew, and everything good inside me told me to get up, to throw a glass of water on him, and to walk out the door.

And I did leave, eventually, but not when the sacred parts of me that valued myself as a woman told me to. I left much later and with him by my side, my heart pounding, my brain muddled, all my thoughts unclear.

After an hour's worth of dining with his intoxicating words, I felt weak, like at any moment I might make a decision I would forever regret.

It was there, outside the restaurant, without the security of the table between us that his hands moved over me and he pressed his lips softly onto mine. Then he offered what he'd come for.

"Come to my house," he whispered. The warmth of his breath tickled my ear, sending a shiver down my spine. "Have sex with me."

My heart pounded outside my chest as his invitation hung between us. Neither of us moved.

We had each come to dinner with our own agendas. His was my body, and mine was my soul. I wanted to hear it, to feel it, to believe it; I wanted someone to tell me I was wanted, that I was enough. Now here was a man offering to give me a cure, even if it was just for one night.

What's the big deal anyway? something inside me questioned. *No one has to know.*

Nathan, sensing my hesitation, whispered his invitation again—stronger, bolder, more insistent this time. Closing my eyes, I exhaled slowly.

I got into my car and began to drive west.

West

Lying in bed later that night, rivers of black tears fell freely, soaking the soft white pillowcase and leaving silent trails down the contours of my face. They waited so patiently for home, and I was glad to finally let them tell their story.

After pulling into my parking space as the sun dipped behind the Rockies in the dullness of dusk, I'd climbed the four flights of stairs to my top-floor apartment and turned the key to my door. Just the sight of my bed did me in as I slid under the cool cotton sheets, alone.

My car had driven west, while Nathan's had gone east. I did not go to his home and I did not have sex with him. Yet I would be lying if I said, in that moment where my chest pounded and my resolve felt weak, there wasn't a part of me that didn't want to go.

But buried deeper, below the surface of those desires, I knew my heart was begging a man to answer questions only God had the power to give. There, in my bed, covers pulled tight around me, my emotions burned— buried, raw, undealt with.

No-shows from Lisa. Draining dates with the cringeworthy and pessimistic. Biting attacks from the finance guy via email. Being stood up by two different guys. Anxious anticipation about meeting Evan in one month. A heart brimming with uncertainty after reading his profile.

And on top of it all? My competitor, my cofounder, my sister, my friend—Lisa—was departing for camp in just a few short days. Soon I'd be back to dating alone.

As a young teenage girl with a mouth full of metal, a tie-dyed scrunchie, and no romantic prospects in sight, the decision to link arms with my fellow Christian girlfriends, united and unanimous that we would save sex for marriage, felt like the easiest decision in the world.

Because, of course, if we followed the rules, then everything would work out for us, right? College first. Meet a godly young man. Guy pursues girl. Graduate. Marry young. Land a career. Buy a home. Raise a family. Live happily ever after.

And, as you know, that nine-step plan did happen for most of my dear family members and childhood friends. Yet despite my wishing, my hoping, my praying, it did not happen for me.

As it turned out, life decisions are not just made once in a middle school diary. Those fierce resolutions a girl adopts in her age of innocence are what the woman she becomes will be forced to reexamine over and over and over again.

I knew a list of dos and don'ts could only carry a girl so far before a moment of weakness tips her over the line she has drawn for herself in the sand. And that's the problem with lines. You can skirt them, dance around them, get a little closer each time.

Yet it was not rules or lines that I craved. Instead, there was something softer, more inviting that called to me that night. The one thing that in its kindness had welled up deep inside me, whispering, inviting me to simply not go on that date in the first place.

Wisdom.

It was the same whisper that said to get up and leave during those two disturbing dates weeks prior. The same whisper that told me searching for

Evan's dating profile would not bring me peace. The whisper that said to trust my heart when daters did not treat me well, instead of excusing their bad behavior and pushing icky feelings down.

Take a few steps back, Jen, wisdom whispered. *Protect your heart; respect yourself. Come, live in the wide-open space that's being offered. A field full of margin, with fewer land mines to trip and fall over. A space offering, room to breathe, overflowing with gifts of forgiveness and grace.*

As my heavy, swollen lids began to close, my breathing steadied, lengthened, and slowed, giving relief to the ache inside my head. Eager for rest, eager to put the evening behind me, eager for the sun to rise again, I fell into the deepest sleep I'd had since the dating challenge began.

Pearls

The next day, I called a trusted friend. She listened quietly as I confessed every word of my last several weeks. Being stood up. The unexpected attack over email. Sitting through a string of dates with men who did not treat me well. Viewing a profile I never should have read. And of course, Nathan.

We talked for a long time about the heartaches that often coexist with dating. After a pause, her voice softened. "You know you've been throwing your pearls to the pigs, right, Jen?"

My chest tightened at her words; tears stung my eyes. I did know, and my only regret was that I had not stood up for myself sooner. Part of how I defined femininity was knowing my value and having a voice.

I wanted to be a woman who stood up for herself when the need arose. A woman who exercised her boundaries. A woman who knew how to sidestep punches—emotionally, mentally, or physically—with maturity, strength, and grace. And, if needed, to be able to throw one back.

Funny enough, in those final days of July, there was only one thing I had left to check off on my list: "#31. Take a self-defense class." And the only one available was at a UFC pro boxing gym across town.

I had no idea what I was in for as the fight club attendants taped my wrists, then pounded big red gloves on each hand and strapped a helmet on my head. That afternoon, I tripped and rolled, whistles blew, my knees got scraped up. I army crawled across cold concrete under swinging punching bags, my gut getting nailed more than once.

Rocky Balboa soundtracks rocked inside my brain as sweat flung through the air, running rivers down my arms, back, and neck. Muscles I didn't know existed wobbled. By the end I was jelly.

And after class I once again drove west. Same rusty car, same paved road, but a very different me.

Dating was not the place to find my identity. It was not the space to get validation or discover my value. I needed to come with a full cup, an overflowing cup. Because without boundaries and a voice, without knowing exactly where my true identity came from, I'd be eaten alive.

Good-byes

"So, this is it, huh, Lis?" It was our final video chat before she left for camp. Behind her, I could see several packed suitcases and a laundry basket full of thrift-store costumes and board games.

Typical Lisa. Things were going to be really different without her in August.

She and I had talked things through. It wasn't an easy conversation for either of us; we'd let one another down in more ways than one.

Though it hurt when we made plans and she forgot, I owned up to the fact that I was not her boss, her mom, or her dating probation officer. Sure, our competition made more sense with her partnership, and it was fun having someone to laugh and trash-talk with. But at the end of the day, at the end of our challenge, the only person I was responsible for was me.

She forgave me too. My hotheaded reactions to her missed calls had been overboard. Over the course of several tough weeks, my stress had become one big knot, and a lot of it had nothing to do with her. I should have taken time to pull apart my frustrations, to identify what I felt and for whom. It had been unfair to blast Lisa, full force, with all my open wounds.

After unpacking our hurts, we decided to finish the challenge but noted that the health of our relationship came before points, before dating. And now we were kick-starting our newest monthly theme: Wiser, Smarter, Stronger. We agreed it was the fresh start we both needed.

I pulled out the pink notebook, ready to review our scoreboard. To my surprise, Lisa pulled out a small notebook too. Sure, it was covered in Teenage Mutant Ninja Turtles, but after our tough conversation, it warmed my heart that she was trying.

When it came time to say good-bye, Lisa stuffed her tiny notebook and a pack of jumbo playing cards into her purse. Her eyes danced. "Can you believe our trip to Glacier is in just four weeks?"

My heart skipped a beat.

"I can't wait, Lis." Though I didn't say his name, we both knew what I meant.

Chapter 13 | Wiser, Smarter, Stronger

"Sometimes, what heart know, head forget."

~ *Mr. Miyagi,* The Karate Kid

"Hey sister! How's camp?" I typed the following Sunday.

My hair was piled into a messy bun and held in place by a soft terry cloth headband. A creamy-white lycopene masque chemically brightened my face, neck, and décolleté. When it came to antioxidants, my motto remained: more is always more.

The getup was part of my new "Sundays at Seven" evening beauty regimen. I planned to spend one hour every Sunday night doing a protein hair treatment, antioxidant facial masque, full-body dry brushing, skin remineralization, aromatic steamed towel, head-to-toe moisturization, and application of vitamin rich serums, peptide eye crème, and stem-cell face crème.

Why yes, I did have more time on my hands now that Lisa was gone. Why do you ask?

Dabbing a little masque from under my eye, I continued typing:

As promised, here's my points. It was an insane travel week, but I managed to squeeze in a few challenges:

- 2 first dates (swipe left) – 25 points/each
- 3 workouts – 10 points/each

- Read 4 chapters in Proverbs – 10 points/each

TOTAL = 120 points

Oh, and I'm going on a 2nd date with your future hubby, Will, this Saturday! Purely platonic of course. My matchmaking skills are going to blow your mind!!!

Sunshine 'n SPF,

Jen

Lisa and I had just started our new monthly theme: Wiser, Smarter, Stronger. There were two ways to earn bonus points in August.

The first was called Couples Therapy. Our plan was to interview married duos we admired, using five strategic, predetermined questions. The goal was to pocket their wisdom, supercharging our own dating lives. As incentive, interviews earned 25 points each.

During my work trip, I had sent out email requests to fifteen married couples I loved and respected. I'd received several responses, but no interview dates were set in stone.

The second way Lisa and I could earn theme points was to read the book of Proverbs, aka "the wisdom book." While gaining knowledge was important to us, we knew that even a cell phone had the power to accumulate raw data and facts. But acquiring wisdom was something different, something special. It was discernment, a penetrating transcendence that could help someone navigate through any stage of life.

When it came to becoming better versions of ourselves, Lisa and I wanted all the wisdom we could get. Topics in the book of Proverbs covered everything from business to wealth, charity to character, politics to sex, friendship to ambition. And, of course, relationships and love. There were thirty-one chapters, one for every day in August. Each earned 10 points.

After emailing Lisa my scoreboard update, I leaned back into the wooden spindles of an old kitchen chair and logged into my student loan account.

Earlier that afternoon, I'd sold my dining buffet on Craigslist; I had no need for it anymore. It cramped my small space, plus, I had been selling all the unused belongings inside it throughout the year. While most of the profits were designated for making a student loan payment, I also added a small portion to my new clothes fund too.

Since April I'd gone on thirty-six dates. And by the looks of my first-date outfit (pilling black Target tank, thinning Old Navy jeans, sagging cardigan buttons, scuffed flats), those numbers were starting to show. It had been eleven months of pounding away at debt, of not buying new things.

But every month I'd been putting a few bucks into a crumpled envelope. Penciled across the top, it read Clothes Budget—savings for a day I'd need it most. After selling the buffet, I now had exactly what I needed to buy a new pair of hiking boots and a fresh first-date outfit.

Scanning my living space, I felt a sense of pride. Decluttering the physical was doing the same inside my soul. Simplifying at home meant less cleaning and organizing, less time stressing over chaos. Even when dating felt like a complicated mess, I breathed easier knowing my closets were not.

I submitted a $150 bonus payment to my Sallie Mae student loans, then typed it into my Debt Payoff Tracker spreadsheet. Tracking was my life now—dates, points, dollars, even pounds on weigh-in Wednesdays. Some weeks showed little to no progress on each goal. But it was amazing to watch how, over time, each teeny-tiny step added up.

By the time I updated my tracker, I had two new emails. One from Lisa, another from my friend Amanda.

Hey Jen!

How are you? Camp is amazing! Erin, Angela, Andrew, Lisa S., Andy, and Kacie all say hi by the way! :) Here's my points this week:

- 7 workouts (daily adventure courses) – 10 points/ each
- 1 mentor meeting in the plum orchard – 10 points

- 4 "meet men" (gotta love camp bachelors) – 50 points/each
- Read 5 chapters of Proverbs (on the Sassy Deck with a chai, wish you were here) – 10 points/each
- 3 poolside Couples Therapy interviews – 25 points/each

TOTAL = 405 points

Waterslides open in ten. Gotta run!

—Lisa

Glancing at my reflection on the screen, I noted my once-creamy masque had hardened like cement, pulling my skin taut like a face-lift gone wrong. Lisa, my worthy adversary, was back in the lead.

Things were quiet without her. I missed our comical text exchanges to stay motivated and encouraged after funny mishaps and dates gone wrong. But I was happy for Lisa too; I knew better than anyone, there was no life like camp life.

The second email was from my friend Amanda: "Hey, Jen! Matt and I would love to help with your Couples Therapy challenge! Can you come over on Wednesday night after the girls go to bed, around eight?"

I couldn't help but laugh at the irony and be encouraged by God's kindness when I read her words. Matt, Amanda, and I had all worked together at the same Young Life camp Lisa was at all month. While my sister traveled over five hundred miles to be surrounded by tight community, I was getting a slice of it in a living room, just one suburb away.

"That's perfect! Can't wait," I responded.

They were an awesome trial couple for me. Matt was all energy and enthusiasm, a go-getter, always up for a new adventure. And Amanda was one of the kindest, most encouraging cheerleaders I knew. Together they were authentic and real—transparent about life, faith, and marriage. In just a few days, Couples Therapy would officially begin.

I'm Already Taken

"Okay, so let me get this straight." Matt grinned, reclining on the couch, his long legs stretched across the ottoman in front of him. "You got points for eating bacon . . . wrapped in bacon?"

It was Wednesday night, and I was sprawled on the living room floor, giving Matt and Amanda a rundown of our competition. Curled at my feet was their yellow lab, Obi, while their three young girls lay tucked in bed down the hall.

The four of us, Obi included, had met nine summers prior at that Young Life camp in Oregon. Back then we were in our midtwenties; Amanda was a year older than I was, and Matt two years older. They'd already been married five years when we met, tying the knot soon after college.

I always admired their teamwork, the way their gifts complemented each other's so well. I was excited to learn more.

To kick things off, I filled them in on the monthly themes, then entertained them with tales of speed dating, the Baby Josh mix-up, and all the one-liners I'd been practicing for five straight months. They were all laughs.

It felt good to share my stories with others. While a small handful of friends knew I was doing some dating experiment with my sister, Lisa and I had not broadcast details until now. It wasn't a secret; we just didn't want too much attention or pressure. We were building the plane while flying it, and wanted to avoid drifting from the deeper work we set out do.

But now, in month five, our stories were out.

Sitting cross-legged at Matt's side, Amanda piped in. "This challenge is seriously cool." She hugged a throw pillow to her chest. "I love that you guys are doing this!" No one could offer sweet reassurance like Amanda. And no one could spark amusement quite like Matt.

"This is where you guys come in," I said. "In August we get points for asking married couples five relationship questions."

"Oh gosh." Amanda shot Matt a look. "I hope we don't fail the test," she joked. I assured her there were no right or wrong answers.

"Matt, the first question is for you," I said, clicking my pen. "Where do you think single women go wrong in their approach with men? What could we do better to speak a guy's language?"

Matt lit up, sharing insight from a recent article in the *Wall Street Journal*. He said it talked about men's desire for women to show interest in their hobbies, and how couples who dove into each other's passions had stronger relationships.

"Amanda will do things that aren't her first choice," he said. "I love it when she tries one of my hobbies, even when I know it's not her thing." And Matt had many hobbies: coaching soccer, beekeeping, home renovating, cycling, gardening, real estate, downhill skiing, building coops for his chickens. It's what everyone loved about Matt; he never did anything halfway.

My mind drifted back to the baseball game during man month. Never had I sparked so much interest from a guy than after my date discovered I'd read *Sports Illustrated* the day prior, and was trying golfing and shooting later that week. What Matt said made sense, though I hadn't had the words until now.

For the next hour, conversation breezed between amusement and depth as we discussed the complexities of relationships. I wrapped up Couples Therapy by asking if there was anything they wanted to add.

Amanda, the eternal cheerleader, tenderly shared, "Just remember you'll never find someone who is perfect . . ."

Flawlessly on cue, Matt puffed his chest. "Because I'm already taken!"

That night we laughed until our faces hurt. *Who needs waterslides when you have nights like this?* I thought, hugging each of them good night.

After ten days without my sidekick, it felt good to be loved. It felt good to be known.

Willingness

The next night, my brother, Brian, and sister-in-law, Ashley, after putting my niece and nephew to bed, appeared on the screen. It didn't take long for laughter to build in the airwaves between us as I explained the competition to another duo, in all its comedies and tragedies.

"But Lisa doesn't even have a dog!" They died at the thought of our sister, in her Super Mario Brothers T-shirt, carrying a huge bag of dog treats, just to get the digits of two single guys.

Ashley and Brian were a great team and fun to interview. Ash was Lisa's age, with lush Joanna Gaines hair. She was the youth pastor at the church my family grew up in, an oldest child, confident leader, and the most organized person I knew.

Brian was less than two years younger than I was and had always been a wise, steady soul. He was six foot three and had clear blue eyes like our dad, warm auburn hair like our mom, freckles like our sisters, and an obsession for the Financial Peace University "baby steps," just like I did.

Though we often geeked out about finances, getting his dating advice never crossed my mind until now. But his answer to the second Couples Therapy question—"What are the most important qualities a single woman should look for in a guy?"—stuck with me, more than anyone else's would.

Brian was thoughtful before sharing that *willingness* was one of the best characteristics to look for in a person. He explained, "When I met Ashley, I wasn't killing it with my finances. I wasn't reading my Bible every day. I knew more video game titles than personal development books. I didn't have a mentor I met with. I couldn't cook; I barely even knew how to make toast."

I'd always considered Brian a stand-up guy. When he met Ashley, he had a solid faith, good friends, volunteered with the youth group, loved our family. But he was right: back in those days, he wasn't as evolved as he was now.

Current Brian was meeting with a mentor each month. He volunteered to teach Financial Peace University. He had a consistent Bible reading habit, a solid work ethic. He did laundry, cleaned bathrooms, was an equal partner around the home.

"I think one of the most important qualities to look for are guys who are willing to self-improve and self-reflect as they move through life," he said.

It made sense. Early on, Brian had shaggy hair and ate Twizzlers for dinner. He didn't start his relationship as the perfect guy, but he did have a humble foundation. From the beginning, he showed a spirit of willingness to become the leader that his community and family needed him to be.

Willingness. It was a refreshing answer that immediately went to the top of my list.

The three of us talked for an hour, hitting all five questions. It was fun conversation and stuff I'd never taken the time to ask them before.

By the time we said good night, I felt inspired to take a deeper look inside myself. Did I have that humble willingness to evolve? Or was I dead set in my ways?

The Slow Simmer

Standing in front of my full-length mirror, I held a new raspberry hip-length tank to my shoulders. I turned side to side, running my fingers over the soft coolness that only new fabrics have. It was Saturday night, and I was excited to try out my new outfit and, of course, my matchmaking skills with Will too.

Clipping the price tag, I slipped on the top and did the same with a new long lightweight buttonless navy cardigan and a fresh pair of jeans. No more saggy buttons, baggy kneecaps, or pilling fabric on the inner thighs. I felt brand spankin' new.

To finish the look, I added a bright multi-colored vintage bangle, a new long pendant necklace, and on-trend booties. My new first-date outfit was nothing fancy or expensive, but I felt fun and playful wearing pops of color instead of basic neutrals and black.

My original plan was to save the ensemble a couple more weeks for my hopeful date in Montana. But I couldn't wait. After months of sacrifice, it felt like an explosion of joy to slip into brand-new, well-fitting clothes. And even sweeter that I had meticulously saved for them, using that envelope of cash.

A month had passed since my first date with Will. He took kids to camp for a week; then I flew out on business. Then he had a family vacation planned. It was no secret our online dating profiles showed active every few days, which meant we were both still putting ourselves out there with new people. Things felt casual, like a slow, simmering Crock-Pot on a Sunday afternoon.

Judging from our handful of brief interactions, I sensed Will was the most stand-up, like-minded Christian guy I'd met all challenge. Heck, if it weren't for the fact that I was taller than he was . . . and Lisa was perfect for him . . . and my hopeful-future-honey-bear Evan wasn't waiting for me up north . . . then maybe . . .

Nah, I thought as I brushed my teeth. He and Lisa shared an uncanny quirky side. She was the shorter, spunkier, simplified version of me. Their equal love for keeping costumes in their trunks "just in case" far superseded mine.

I, on the other hand, was planned and strategic. Tall, a deep feeler. Frugal, yet frivolous. When it came to emotions, emojis, and lip gloss, I was super-duper extra. There was simply no doubt in my mind which guy was meant for each girl.

Evan, the vertically gifted business leader, is more my type, I determined, grabbing my keys and heading out the door. And I was certain that Will—the short, energetic math goofball—was everything Lisa never knew she always wanted.

Second Date

Will and I settled into an oversized booth in the middle of a steakhouse for coffee and dessert. The lights were dim, the ceilings tall, and all the décor rustic and ornate.

"Great to see you again, Jen!" His booming baritone matched the grandeur of the room. Will's ensemble was simple: dad-bod blue jeans, a worn-in gray button-up, smart frames, a dated watch, worn brown leather shoes, average build, slightly balding. Passing me a dessert menu, he flashed an oversized grin.

I felt different that night. Maybe it was the way my new lightweight sweater hung from my frame, or maybe it was because my skin and hair felt soft and hydrated, thanks to my new rockin' Sunday night self-care routine.

Perhaps it was the fact that I'd hit a personal milestone that morning by jogging three miles in my neighborhood, then walking two more. Or that I'd paid off another student loan the day prior. Maybe it was the joy bubbling inside me after a few rounds of Couples Therapy. Or the way my Bible's bookmark had been steadily moving through Proverbs.

Whatever it was, I couldn't have held it back if I tried.

Will and I talked like we'd known one another for years. I discovered he found my profile on Match by searching Christian author names he loved. It turned out, like me, Will was an avid reader and podcast nerd. We enjoyed a lot of the same stuff.

Just as I was about to pull out Cupid's bow and arrow, thrilling him with details of Lisa, Will threw me for a loop.

"How tall are you?" There was a twinkle in his eye as he took a bite of cheesecake.

"Taller than you," I teased. I couldn't believe it; his question was the perfect tee-up for my grand matchmaking plan. *Lisa + Will 4 Ever*, I thought.

"No way! I'm definitely taller." Tossing his linen napkin on the table, he stood and called our waitress. "Theresa! We need your help."

Resting my elbow on the table, I ducked my head down, using my hand to shield my face. Will didn't seem to mind that a few heads had turned.

Slipping off his shoes in the middle of the steakhouse, he flashed his classic oversized grin. "Stand up, Jen. Take off your shoes."

Theresa, our waitress, aka Will's new bestie, was into it. After some coaxing, I stood red-faced in just my socks, back to back with Will next to our booth. The tables around us looked entertained.

Placing her hand flat across the tops of our heads, Theresa studied us. Then she announced the verdict. "Yep. You're almost the same height. But he is a little taller!" The couple in the booth next to ours responded in agreement. The guy flashed a thumbs-up, while the girl gave an emphatic nod.

I glanced down to make sure Will wasn't standing on a thick-cut sirloin or a basket of fries, but there wasn't so much as a napkin under his toes.

Pulling my shoes back on, I slid into the booth. "Fine!" I said. "You win, Mr. Five-Foot-Ten-and-One-Quarter-Inch."

As we redirected back to dessert and conversation, I couldn't help but notice Will looked . . . different. *Has he been working out?* I wondered, scoping out his arms.

And sure enough, when we stood to leave, he seemed a little taller too.

Chapter 14 | Couples Therapy

"Walk with the wise and become wise."

~ King Solomon, approximately 900 BC

A few days later, I closed my car door on College Avenue in Fort Collins, an hour north of Denver. Stepping onto the sidewalk, I joined my friends Erik and Alyssa for a stroll to a little hole-in-the-wall lunch spot for another round of Couples Therapy.

I met them in that coed church life group when I first moved to Denver, four years prior. They were dating at the time; both tall, dark, attractive. I instantly fell in love with their artistic, linguistic, and deep souls, perfectly layered with fun and adventurous sides.

Both in their thirties when they married, they recalled broken engagements to other people before they met and their story began. Because of this, I was particularly interested in their responses to the third Couples Therapy question.

"If you could go back in time and do your dating years all over again, what would you do differently? Is there anything you'd keep the same?" I clarified the question wasn't targeted at their dating relationship with one another, but their individual years in general.

Erik sat introspective, then shared how much he enjoyed cultivating his hobbies and interests. He had studied languages and had lived in

Alaska, the Midwest, Costa Rica, and Mexico. Instead of spending his single years with a "when I meet someone, then I'll *xyz*" attitude, he made the decision early on not to wait for *someday* for life to begin.

Alyssa nodded as he talked. She, too, had a passion for languages and living in foreign countries. She did not waste her single years. Instead, she cultivated hobbies that made her come alive: writing, swimming, teaching, traveling. Their passions were major connection points when they were eventually set up by mutual friends.

Their stories sparked my memory of hobbies I loved but in adulthood had slowly lost. Canoeing on still, glassy waters in northern Minnesota, the land of 10,000 Lakes. Taking new business courses and art classes. Road trips while jamming to music and podcasts, destination anywhere. Content creation, writing, creative projects. Hospitality and enjoying good food around my table with dear friends.

As I drove home that afternoon, I reflected on Erik and Alyssa's golden years of self-discovery, both earning master's degrees and deepening their faiths. Each of them had viewed singleness as a gift to be explored, not a prison cell to survive.

I loved their reminder that exploring and discerning things that make us come alive as individuals wasn't *in* the way of love. But *on* the way.

Expectations

"All right, next question," I said to my longtime friends, Jon and Ann Marie, through my screen.

Ann Marie and I met in middle school and shared countless sleepovers, boat days at her family's lake place, youth group retreats, and homemade ice cream blizzards. The sweet but fiery redhead met her baseball-and-bass-fishing-loving husband in college, so I'd known him over a decade too. They married shortly after graduation, with me wearing gold satin at her side.

"This question is just for you, Ann Marie. Were there any expectations you had going into marriage that ended up being unrealistic?"

Without missing a beat, she raised a brow and flashed a joking side-eyed "look" at Jon. "I don't feel like my expectations were unrealistic, babe."

His eyes widened in mock innocence, raising his hands as if to surrender. "Hey! What are you guys looking at me for?"

We all laughed. Jon wrapped his arm around Ann Marie's shoulders, then kissed her forehead. Her answer reminded me of a comment in Matt and Amanda's interview.

"There's a reason rom-coms don't show what happens after the couple falls in love," Matt had said. Even though we knew movies didn't portray reality, the dream of "happily ever after" was still a unicorn Lisa and I dreamed of.

Digging into relationship expectations was not totally designed to crush our hopes for romance and butterflies. But we wanted to get real with ourselves. Put simply, we were asking couples to tell us more about the part where love became a verb, not just a feeling.

Pastor Tim Keller puts it this way in his book *The Meaning of Marriage*: "Single people cannot live their lives well as singles without a balanced, informed view of marriage. If they do not have that, they will either over-desire or under-desire marriage, and either of those ways of thinking will distort their lives."[1]

Lisa and I knew it would serve us well to adjust our lenses. Neither dating nor marriage existed to fulfill our rose-colored fantasies. Both took hard work.

"Okay, let me rephrase my question," I said as Jon winked through the screen. "How was marriage glamorized for you before your wedding, and how did that compare to the reality of marriage?"

"You know my dad, Jen," Ann Marie said. "Growing up, we went on breakfast dates every Saturday after early morning runs. It was our thing.

---

1   Tim Keller, *The Meaning of Marriage: Facing the Complexities of Commitment with the Wisdom of God* (New York: Penguin Books, 2011), pg219.

For whatever reason, I always imagined my husband and I would do all the same stuff, and in the same way, as my dad and I did."

Leaning into Jon, she continued. "I had to figure that one out. It was tempting to look to Jon to fill me up when and how I needed it." But after time, she said she began to appreciate the ways Jon cared for her, though they were different from her dad's ways.

"Marriage has taught me not to play the comparison game, to let Jon be his own man."

I understood what Ann Marie was saying. Even in dating, it was tempting to compare new guys to my dad or brother, my friends' husbands, or relationships from the past. It was also easy to fantasize that marriage would solve everything.

Couples Therapy with Jon and Ann Marie told me to ditch the comparison game. To let a guy be himself. And to carry a balanced, informed view of marriage, remembering it's not meant to fix and patch all our raggedy single edges.

Hold It Loosely

"All right, Mom and Dad, last question," I announced over FaceTime.

My mom's iPad sat on my parents' antique formal dining table in the rural 1960s ranch house I grew up in. Through the screen, I saw nostalgia and stability. They had been married well over thirty years, though I'd never spent time digging into their success.

Dad's silver hair matched his goatee, his blue eyes set against his tanned skin. He wore his usual "working in the yard" attire: a black quick-dry shirt and dark-gray cargo shorts. I didn't have to see his feet to know he wore white midcalf socks with white New Balance shoes.

Mom was put together, per the usual, her hazel eyes behind new on-trend glasses and her auburn hair curled, volumized, then sprayed to perfection. As always, her gold drop earrings coordinated with both her necklace and a stylish top in olive green.

Like most kids, I undervalued my parents when I was growing up. But now, as an adult, I knew they were better than gold. There was no other marriage I'd observed so closely, so clearly. For over three decades, I had a front row seat to the commitment, the forgiveness, the resilience, the patience, the hurts, the laughs, the till-death-do-we-part kind of love my parents had.

I was lucky, and I knew it.

We'd finished the first four questions and had only one left. It was the only question I felt nervous to ask each couple. For some reason, I feared being chastised for living my single years all wrong. But so far in Couples Therapy, my vulnerability was only met with kindness, and I had no reason to believe it would change now.

"All right, Mom and Dad. In what ways do you think singles are too picky?"

They sat thoughtfully for a moment; then my mom shared. "I think it's good to be picky!" My dad said he agreed.

It was nearly the exact same response every couple had given: a pause, followed by two simple words, "Be picky!" Apparently, successful matches felt selectivity was a wise first step in choosing a lifelong mate.

My parents, along with every other couple, expanded the conversation. Equally as important as their advice to be picky came additional insights of what they learned to let go.

"I think it's important to make a list of qualities you want," my mom explained. "But then to hold that list loosely. What are really, really the nonnegotiables?"

My dad said the book of Proverbs was a good place to start, advising us how to live. I smiled as he talked; he had no idea Lisa and I were reading through it for points. "Is a man seeking God? And does he treat others well?" he continued. "Those are what matter most."

A few days prior, my friends Jay and Erin answered by saying there was no such thing as The One. No *perfect fit*, *soul mate*, or *you complete me*. "Burn that to the ground," Jay had said. "Every couple will have stuff to go through."

Seven different individuals thought too much weight was put on first impressions. Too much pressure for a first date to go well or to find someone with all the same hobbies and interests.

Amanda had said, "Somebody could see Matt for ten-minute windows in different stages of his day and get ten different ideas of who he is." Her point was that second, third, or more dates could give a richer picture of an amazing person. Qualities that truly matter for the long haul aren't always caught on first dates.

Another person commented that singles often let one impression of someone define who they believe that person to be.

One husband advised me to prioritize deal breakers. Don't move on so quickly over changeable things, like bad breath (gum, anyone?) or a fashion faux pas. "True deal breakers," he'd said, "should have more to stand on than that."

It seemed there were two things everyone unanimously agreed on. First, be picky. And second, don't get too attached to a list of preconceived notions about what the final package should look like. Though I tried to avoid it, Evan flashed through my mind.

As my parents and I wrapped up our interview, I felt encouraged, not just in dating but in singleness too. My folks always encouraged me to run hard and fast in my lane, to make the most of this life and my gifts.

Their greatest victory as parents wasn't for their kids to get married. It was for them to know the Lord and to become wiser, smarter, and stronger each step of the way.

Needing People

Sitting at a small table the following night, I watched Rob, a new date, nervously spin the cardboard sleeve on his empty cup. Imprinted on his left ring finger was the faded indentation of a thick wedding band.

As he looked at me, I could tell he wished he was looking at her. His heavy shoulders gave way to the weight of sitting across from the first woman he'd gone out with, besides his bride, in over fifteen years.

Eleven months prior, his wife had lost her battle to an aggressive form of breast cancer, shattering his world and that of their three young kids he cared for alone. Tired eyes hinted at a heart gasping for air, as he worked all day, then searched cupboards for sippy cups and a box of mac 'n cheese, consoling broken cries, praying to make it through one more night.

I was his first date since she'd passed. His first online date ever. "A lot has changed since then," he confided. The last first date he'd had was during his freshman year in college; he was just nineteen years old.

From the moment we shook hands, it was as if an unspoken agreement hung between us. One in which I would play an important role for him, and he would play an important role for me.

He needed what I had to offer: kindness, grace, space to practice a new stage of life. He needed to get through a new first, needed to practice buying a cup of coffee, practice sitting across from someone new. Needed to practice listening and asking and caring and hoping.

In that moment, I knew Rob did not need a new wife. He did not need a new mom for his kids. He knew, as well as I did, he just needed to survive sitting in that chair without totally falling apart. And I was honored to help him do so.

I was struck by the unexpected place Rob found himself in. He confessed that until his wife passed, he hadn't needed much from other people. Yet now he needed help from family to care for his three young kids. He needed meals when he could barely get out of bed. He needed borrowed strength from friends so that he, in turn, could hold his household together.

Hanging on his every word, I knew I was being forever changed. For as long as I could remember, I had been afraid to need. *Nobody wants to be labeled as needy,* I'd always thought. It was a word used to describe the clingy, the anxious, the insecure.

Despite people's purest intentions, *need* has become a curse word. An acidic four letters reserved for clingers and dependents.

Culturally, finding independence, in my experience, had always been encouraged. Promoted even. My entire adulthood had been a series of steps toward self-reliance, each one giving me less and less reason to need other people. For better or for worse, I had achieved what I set out to do.

Bake the cookies, pay the bills, load the bikes, wear the lipstick. Carry the boxes, caulk the shower, fix the flat, iron the clothes. Work the job, wash the laundry. Make the bacon, bring home the bacon. Kill the scary spider, jump the car, shave the legs, paint the trim. Shovel the snow, dust the shelves, wear the apron . . . and wear the pants.

Through the years, I often wished for someone else to partner on that list with. It wasn't my first choice to sit on the floor alone, surrounded by piles of Ikea boards, while dinner boiled over on the stove. But years of flying solo had spun their own story. And with time, the only life I knew was one on my own.

Driving home after my date, I reflected on the difficult place Rob found himself in. With a vulnerability he'd never tapped into before, he was allowing himself to ask for help. He was inviting others into his story.

As I pulled into my parking lot, my phone rang. It was Rob. He called to let me know he wasn't ready to start dating quite yet, but it was a blessing to be greeted with kindness on his first try. I could sense the genuine gratitude in his tired voice, and I felt honored to have been the one to help him step forward on his journey.

A new thought tugged inside as we wished one another well. *What if the greatest gift we could give another soul was to simply need them?* Rob had done that for me. It blessed me to bless.

Nothing about him seemed needy, though he'd accepted help all year. Needing people, it seemed, was different than needy people.

In August, Couples Therapy had been my Lisa—my cheering squad on a solo journey that sometimes felt hard. After a month of pulling people in tight, of collecting their stories and confessing mine, my heart was really, really full.

After meeting Rob, I knew my greatest wins that month had little to do with our scoreboard. It was good to practice needing people, to allow others to rally and support me.

Though it felt unnatural asking for help, I knew how much it filled my cup to love on others. It would be good for me to keep practicing vulnerability, to have needs, and to give others the gift of being needed as well.

Collective Wisdom

Pulling the cap off a yellow highlighter, I sat on my bed, surrounded by a month's worth of interview notes. August was wrapping up. That morning, Lisa was back in cell range, which meant I was back to blowing up her phone with every thought, emotion, experience, and feeling backlogged in my brain during her time at camp.

"Couples Therapy is everything," I texted her. Channeling my inner influencer, I included a flat lay photo of my white cotton duvet, covered in wrinkled papers, sticky notes, laptop, and markers in every color of the rainbow. My trusty notebook was no longer simply pages of points. It was a living, breathing binder packed with wisdom from the men and women who had gone before me.

Warm afternoon rays filtered through my blinds as I worked. Pushing the tip of my highlighter across papers, I watched words unite into one powerful voice. Themes lifted off pages as I scribbled notes, poured over answers, and tapped across keys.

By the time the Colorado sun faded to dusk, I had my pièce de résistance. One master chart of top answers, packed with wisdom and encouragement from family and friends.

"If you could go back in time and do the dating thing all over again," I'd asked, "what would you do differently?" Almost everyone said they'd have more fun, feel less pressure, be more relaxed. Stop overanalyzing, not attach so quickly—be less emotional about the process altogether.

A lot of people said they'd be friends first and friends longer. Some regretted staying in the wrong relationship too long. Most said they wished they'd spent more time exploring life as an individual. Others said they would have been less physical, wished they'd waited for sex, been more confident in themselves.

When I asked the guys the question, "What things could women do differently in their approach to men?" I couldn't write fast enough.

Almost all of those solid, stand-up Christian men said the same thing: be confident, be authentic, be who you are. Over and over, they reiterated that their hope was that women wouldn't feel the need to change themselves for some guy. Truly good men, they shared, want to see the women in their lives loving themselves—secure and confident in who they are.

They encouraged women to be their own person, and to let guys be their own person too. Respect, of course, was important to pretty much all the guys. Men can be fragile and sensitive, they shared. So cheering them on meant a lot.

They also said, "Forgive us. Sometimes we're clueless, but don't misread that as thinking we don't care." Because when it comes to good guys, they really, really do.

Next, I'd asked my female friends, "Were there any expectations you were given about marriage that ended up being unrealistic?" Every single one of them laughed.

A few girlfriends shared that after years of dreaming about marital bliss, they were surprised to discover it was actually quite hard. One said she knew it was work for everyone else; she just believed she'd be the exception. Another half-joked that she thought marriage was when mind reading would start.

Many said they anticipated spending all their time together. Some expected conflicts and bad habits would change or be less annoying once they tied the knot. All of my women friends and family members loved and cherished their men, but I appreciated their vulnerability in sharing the tough parts of marriage too.

"What qualities should I look for in a guy?" I asked both men and women. The husbands told me to look for a guy who has healthy relationships in his life, someone who values family and Christ. They also said he should have grit and morals. Chemistry was important too.

The ladies said look for a Christ follower, for a man who has similar vision for his life as my own. Integrity, leadership, and motivation were high on their list. And definitely, they said, look for someone you can have fun and laugh with.

More than anything, Couples Therapy reminded me that healthy and whole relationships always start with healthy and whole singles. I was reminded there is beauty from ashes. And I was reminded great relationships were not only worth the work; they were also worth the wait.

Nervcited

The next morning, still in my pajamas, I tossed my suitcase on my bed. One by one, I folded each piece of my new first-date outfit.

Raspberry-red, hip-length tank—*check.*

Long, gauzy, lightweight navy sweater—*check.*

New pair of jeans—*check.*

Long pendant and large vintage bangle—*check.*

Then I gathered my other essentials. Favorite lip gloss, a large-barrel curling iron, a pair of faux diamond stud earrings, and several pairs of shoes. Each item was neatly zipped, tucked, and packed.

After packing up the rest of my clothes and all our camping gear, there was just one thing left. Picking up a polka-dotted, gift-wrapped box tied with a bright red bow, I slipped it into a paper grocery sack. Then I set it gently into my suitcase and zipped the whole thing shut.

The trip I had been waiting for had finally arrived. Opening a group thread on my phone, I texted Lisa and Emily. "This is really happening! I can't believe I get to see you beauties tomorrow night!"

My heart fluttered as I glanced at my suitcase. I wasn't sure if I was nervous or excited or perhaps a little bit of both. The truth was, I hadn't been that nervcited in years.

Chapter 15 | Glacier

"You miss 100 percent of the shots you don't take."

~ ~~Wayne Gretzky~~ *Michael Scott*

We arrived in Montana, one by one, late the next night. Lisa, by car from Idaho, an eight-hour drive. Emily, by flight from Arizona, with a two-hour layover in Salt Lake. And me, road tripping from Denver with fifteen hours to rehearse what I'd say when I called Evan the next day.

After 864 minutes of diligent strategizing, "Hi" was all I had.

Lisa lived in Montana for three years after college and still had great community there. One of her good friends was graciously hosting us the nights we weren't camping.

Pulling into the long pitch-black driveway just past midnight, I stared in awe at the stars blanketing the western-country sky. The air was mountain fresh and icy cold; only a band of crickets broke the night silence. As I stood to stretch, my interior light illuminated a packed-out car: sleeping bags, a four-man tent, a double-burner cookstove, pots, and pans.

Just then, the front door burst open. I could see the black outlines of two women exploding off the front stoop toward me. They tackled me in the driveway, creating a long run in the nude nylons I still wore from my work meeting in northern Colorado that morning.

Each of us talked a mile a minute, bouncing topics in hushed voices, our arms loosely linked together. "How was your flight? How were your drives? Beds are ready for us downstairs. I brought Uno! Is that a new fleece? Look at your blonde hair, hottie! Which coffee shop are we going to in the morning? Yes, I brought bug spray. And sunscreen. Um, confession: we're going to need more trail mix . . ."

Our sister trifecta, together at last.

Here Goes Nothing

The next morning, dew still on the ground and breath visible in the chilly northwest air, Lisa, Emily, and I crammed ourselves and all our gear into my car, then drove to the local market for firewood and food.

It had been eight months since Christmas in Minnesota when our trio was last together. A lot had changed since then.

Emily was settled into her new post-college life in Flagstaff, Arizona, after graduating with a psych degree in Indiana. The last time we'd seen her, she had a sandy-colored pixie cut. It made her look like a really pretty Justin Bieber, which is why we had started calling her The Biebs.

Her hair was now grown into a soft chin-length golden blonde bob, lightened by her summer job working as a wilderness therapist in the high-desert sun. Every other week she commuted five hours to Utah in her little 1998 Honda Civic without a muffler, working eight days on, then six days off.

She was a bronzed goddess from head to toe, making her white teeth and freckles pop under a teal Great Pacific Iron Works trucker hat. I noticed the way she carried herself seemed more grown-up too. Turning twenty-four, then moving west, had stretched her little Bieber wings and let her fly.

After a month at camp, Lisa's skin was freckled and golden too. Her dark mocha hair mixed with strands of silver hung in a long side braid under a navy-and-white ball cap stamped Idaho.

Thanks to our Level Up workout challenge, she had started light, intermittent walk/jogs in April. Five months later, she was now running three to five miles a few days a week, and she was down ten pounds since our challenge began.

Lisa was on cloud nine as she led Emily and me down each aisle in the grocery store of her old stomping grounds. We walked behind her as she greeted each customer like she owned the place, bouncing along with that infamous twinkle in her eyes.

I pushed the cart, all business and roughly eight shades paler than both of them, wearing a Colorado trucker hat and soft Kelly-green Marmot fleece that hadn't fit in years.

The three of us stuck close, checking ingredients off our list for quinoa cakes, citrus salmon, French toast, peach cobbler, and s'mores. "Just the essentials," we joked, tossing in dark roast, garlic cloves, and goat cheese, then Spanish chocolate, scallions, and figs.

After buying enough groceries to last the year, we pushed our loaded cart through the sliding glass doors. Outside, I felt a hand slip into the pocket of my fleece.

"Here," Lisa said. "Call him." Without another word, she walked away. Following Emily's lead, they began Tetris-packing the car.

I stood outside the entrance and pulled out a crumpled receipt. Written on the back was a 10-digit number. There was no name, but I knew whose it was. A wave of mixed emotions settled over me.

Lisa said she had talked me up in the past, had mentioned to him our compatibility a dozen times, though she was fuzzy what was said and when. All I knew was that Lisa seemed confident in her matchmaking abilities. And I was as ready as I'd ever been.

Here goes nothing, I thought.

After what felt like a million rings, the recording started. My cheeks warmed and heart pounded. My mind raced for the perfect words to say.

So . . . I've read a lot about you, I thought. No, not that. *Sorry your LinkedIn profile had 697 hits last month, but I'm hiring for a husband and your resume is a perfect match.* No. Just, no.

My thoughts were interrupted with a *BEEP*.

"Hi, Evan. This is Jen, um, Lisa's sister. She mentioned we should meet sometime, and I'm actually in town for a few days. I'd love to grab a cup of coffee while I'm here. Give me a call and we'll set something up. My number is . . ."

I gave him my number and avoided asking him to have my babies, both of which I felt super proud of. I also mentioned my cell service might be spotty in the park, so I'd return his voice mail on Sunday.

Now only one question remained: *Is he interested?* A car honked, interrupting my thoughts. Lisa and Emily were bumping the horn and pumping the bass.

"Let's get this show on the road!" they shouted. Leaving the weight of that question behind me, I jumped behind the wheel, and we headed north into the majestic peaks of Glacier National Park.

Adventure

Time stood still for three whole days, each one more restful, more life-giving than the last.

Our first morning, gung-ho and full of motivation, we awoke early, hiking to a hidden glacial lake at the top of a peak. We spent the entire afternoon wading emerald waters, snapping photos, and playing frisbee on the rocky shore.

The second day, it drizzled, but undeterred, we put on rain gear and explored, climbing over mossy rocks and broken timbers through an enchanting foggy forest. That afternoon, high on gluttonous amounts of trail mix and fruit leather, we strummed air guitars and made goofy music videos in the misty rain.

After dark, the glow from orange embers danced across our cheeks as we poked sticks into the snaps and crackles of our fire. It was in that sacred circle that laughter melted to conversation, and then confession, unearthing deeper narratives we had each come to explore.

For the first time, Emily fully absorbed the dating challenge Lisa and I had created after her Friday night phone call back in college. We shared how her words started a domino effect in our lives, inspiring us to take a hard look at how we were spending our single years.

We told her about competing for a championship title. And how, between the two of us, we'd been on almost sixty dates in five months.

I shared all the ways I was working to get unstuck, to move toward healthier patterns in life. Emotion welled inside me as I admitted that it was about so much more than dating. Mine was also a journey toward freedom, financial stability, courage, and self-love.

"You're my sage, Em," I said.

She was quiet as she listened. In all honesty, I couldn't believe we'd waited so long to tell her about our challenge. Yet I knew my goal had been to protect her from feeling left out.

The three of us sat watching curls of smoke and sparks spin into the milky night sky. Then Emily began untangling her feelings out loud.

She was more than six years younger than Lisa, eight behind Brian, and over ten years younger than I was. For her entire life, she felt like she was watching from the sidelines, coveting and yearning for the experiences her older siblings lived.

Feeling a million years behind had always been her greatest wound. Yet that night, in her kindness, her wisdom, her grace, Emily shared that since finishing college, she was beginning to see a new perspective. All those years she spent being so caught up in catching up meant she hadn't seen the whole truth.

When Emily was in middle school, then high school and college, she had imagined Lisa and I were spending our twenties and thirties in nonstop adventure. "What I didn't see was that you were each going through a lot of uncertain and hard times too."

It made sense to her why a dating challenge was created. And why, in all her collagen and college hotness (my words, not hers), she would have been a mismatched contender against us, her couch-ridden, spinster older sisters. (Again, my words.)

It was hard being the youngest by that many years, but Emily wasn't a kid anymore. And she had come to heal that wound.

Bending down in the dirt, she held her beanie on, gently blowing the coals to rekindle the flames. I snapped a few nearby sticks and tossed them into the ring.

Cupping a mug of cocoa, Lisa cleared her throat; she shared next. As the middle sister, she was known as go-with-the-flow, lighthearted, easy to please. She shared she never minded growing up in my shadow or being a sidebar to the admiration of our uber-talented Em.

Yet when we chose Montana, her old stomping grounds for our trip, something sparked. It felt like Emily and I had finally purchased tickets to her show. It was her turn to be the hero, the big cheese, our head honcho, El Capitán.

Overnight, Lisa went from daydreamer to trailblazer. She found us a crash pad, lined up all the best coffee shops, showed off her favorite market in town. She led us to a prime camping cove, the path to a secret glacial lake, and scheduled a guy to deliver three bikes to the park the next day.

"I've loved planning this trip for you guys," she said, scrunching her shoulders like she was giving herself a big hug.

The look on her face was simple and bright, like she had waited a lifetime for the moment her curtain would open and she'd get her chance to shine. Lisa didn't mind her place in the middle. Yet she felt so happy taking center stage for the audience that mattered to her the most.

Temperatures had dropped into the thirties by this point, our breath curling between us. But we were Minnesota Swedes, for goodness' sake; a little frostbite never bothered us.

"What about you, Jen?" Em asked, pulling a Swiss Army knife and partially whittled wooden spoon from her pack. It was a project she'd started midsummer around campfires as a wilderness therapy guide.

I watched as small wood shavings flicked off her blade, carving and chipping around handle and head. A creator shaping her creation. Softening edges. Giving form and design to the lifeless, with a greater purpose and vision in mind.

I began by sharing that my greatest joys in life were dreaming big dreams and chasing down goals. Checking things off a list, conquering pursuits, developing people, ideas, and things—these were what made me come alive.

But as a firstborn, there was a dark side that came with it, like perfectionism, high expectations, overwhelming pressure to hit home runs and succeed. The thought of not measuring up or my dreams not going as planned were the kind of blows to knock me off my feet.

That night, I laid my insecurities on the table, confessing them to my sisters out loud. I was one day away from putting the grand finale on a four-year tale, for better or worse, once and for all. And all those self-doubts I thought were cured had returned, crushing and pulling me down again . . .

Will I be chosen? Am I enough? Or are my fears right, and I am simply too much?

Wrapped in blankets and beanies, they listened quietly, giving space for my fears to unfold.

After I confessed it all, their voices rallied around me. Those anxious questions were smoke and mirrors in their eyes. To them I had always been chosen. Had always been their beloved firstborn leader. Had always been exactly enough.

Scattered throughout the west, Lisa, Emily, and I lived very different lives. Yet as the final curls of smoke faded into the starry Montana sky, our ages, stages, and lifestyles no longer mattered.

Deep in our cores, we had bonded over one common thread, fleshed out by three different people in three different ways. Much like Em's half-whittled wooden spoon, we were being formed, carved, and fashioned. Our Creator, shaping his creation, all with greater purpose and vision in mind.

As we climbed into deep piles of down-feathered sleeping bags and as my sisters' breathing fell into the rhythms of sleep, thoughts of Evan lingered inside me.

Has he returned my call? What is waiting for me on the other side of the mountain? I had spent nearly a year becoming someone I was proud of. But was that person enough?

My thoughts shifted to Will, and I softened. He was not in the plan; he wasn't my type . . . was he? Yet the more time we spent together, the more I found myself hoping that Evan was as kind and endearing as he was.

Tossing and turning, I wavered between contradicting thoughts. Evan and Will. Between those truths my sisters spoke into me and the undeniable pressure reemerging inside me. Finally, my breathing slowed into tandem with theirs and I fell asleep.

Fearless

The next day was Sunday. The plan was to make breakfast, pack up camp, then spend the morning on old single-speed cruiser bikes touring the park. We'd wrap up our final adventure with a picnic by a clear glacial lake. Then we'd head to town, shower, and get ready for a local barn dance.

That morning, we raced our bikes, exploring quiet hills buried deep in the national park. I felt eight years old again—that age of innocence, of carefree laughter, where adventure and mystery lurk around every corner in the best possible way. Zigzagging back and forth, we rounded a sharp corner in single file. Emily, then Lisa, then me.

Amusement was clipped short by Emily's echo through the canyons. "Whoa-oa-oa!" Her bike rolled to a stop in front of us. Pulling up behind her, Lisa and I saw why.

With feet planted on the pavement just shy of the road rolling down into a steep drop-off, we stood high above the tree line, enchanted by the panoramic view. Fresh-fallen snow glittered peaks around us, beauty like I'd never seen it before. Tall, rugged pines, a million years old, were painted across a bright blue sky that never seemed to end. Purple peaks with dramatic drops shot up in every direction.

But it was not just the landscape that took my breath away. I watched as Emily, then Lisa pushed off, flying down the hill, howling in delight as they picked up speed. Their legs stuck straight out on either side, no footwork required.

Rolling my front tire up to the edge, I drew in a breath. Then I pushed off. Right foot. Left foot. Right foot. Left foot. Four pedal strokes were all it took to get the momentum I needed.

Wind whipped my soft green fleece, pressing it against my body. My ponytail loosened around my shoulders. Faster and faster, wobbling as I picked up speed, I felt a spark ignite inside me. Steadying the handlebars with a white-knuckled grip, I planted my feet against the pedals, pushing myself up to a standing position.

In that moment, I was transported to a moment at eight years old when I flew down a hill on my banana-seat bike, totally on top of the world. Culotte shorts, a toothy smile, purple star-shaped earrings, pink jelly shoes. Flowery basket, streamers, neon beads on every spoke. A time in which I loved every ounce of my quirky little self—not for anything I'd done but just for the simple purity of who I was.

Now scenery blurred as I flew down the mountainside, yet my internal world felt crystal clear. No competition, no makeup, no pressure to measure up. Just a kid on a bike. Fearless. Brave. Enough.

Pressing myself higher into the wind, I let out a loud, echoing *whoop!* I felt free.

Chapter 16 | Four-Year Dreams

"Do you ever look at someone and wonder what is going on inside their head?"

~ *Joy,* Inside Out

Gentle melodies from Emily's singer-songwriter playlist drifted through my car, setting the mood as we began our final descent out of Glacier National Park late Sunday afternoon. Winding down the pine-covered peaks, we drove in silence, drinking in the majestic panorama.

As we reached the exit, cell towers came into range and three days of messages lit up our phones. *Ding! Ding! Ding!* My stomach flipped as Emily and Lisa checked theirs. I continued to drive.

Pulling into Lisa's recommended rest stop and café, we hopped out to stretch and grab some food before heading into town to shower and go to a barn dance for Emily's final night. Lisa and I would stay in town a couple extra days for her thirtieth birthday party and to plan out our final monthly theme.

"Be right there!" I called after them, clutching my phone inside my red windbreaker pocket. My heart beat a little faster as I smoothed my thumb over the screen before dialing voice mail.

"You have four new messages," the robotic voice replied. "First message."

I paced the parking lot, listening to a lengthy alert from Nancy, my elderly neighbor, regarding a silver Toyota 4Runner parked in my reserved space Friday afternoon. It left me unconcerned.

Next were two chipper voice mails from friends, popping in to say hello.

"Next message," the recording came again. There was a pause followed by a gentleman clearing his throat.

"This message is for Jan. Are you paying too much for your car insurance? For a limited time, receive a quote by calling 1-888 . . ."

My hand dropped to my side. A breeze blew against my two long braids under Emily's borrowed teal trucker hat.

He didn't call.

What-Ifs

Inside the café, I ate my soup and sandwich, pretending like a million questions weren't fumbling through my mind. *That's it? I'm supposed to just move on?*

What if he was out of town? Or I'd dialed the wrong number? What if, just like a '90s rom-com, he'd been in an accident and was now in a coma and I needed to pretend I was his fiancé that he didn't remember because of selective amnesia?

Maybe his house was robbed in the night and they'd stolen his phone. Or he dropped it while saving a Radio Flyer wagon of toddlers stranded in the middle of a busy street! What if he had laryngitis? Or in a fluke, he was stung by a swarm of bees, his fingers too swollen to text?

There were so many likely scenarios, it was hard to land on just one. When Emily and Lisa asked if I'd heard from him, I tightened my lips and shook my head, brushing it off as no big deal.

He'll call, I reassured myself. *There's still time.* But deep inside, uncertainty continued to rise.

The Birthday

"Excited for your big bash, Lis?" I asked the next night as we made our way toward the laughter, lawn games, and heat rising off a sizzling grill.

It was Monday night, Lisa's thirtieth birthday party at her good friend's place. Emily flew back to Arizona that morning after an epic night of spinning circles to "Cotton-Eyed Joe," kicking up dirt and yellow straw. And I still hadn't heard from Evan.

"I'm so excited to see everyone!" she said. Lisa wore a floral blouse, topknot, and sparkly teal earrings, carrying the salad we'd made that afternoon. I was in my new first-date outfit and loose, wavy curls, clutching a polka-dotted gift-wrapped box tied with a bright red bow.

After hugging all her good friends, the festivities began. *Forget Evan,* I coached myself, grabbing a spot at the volleyball net. Tonight was about Lisa.

For the next forty minutes, I bumped, served, set, blocked, spiked, volleyed, passed, power tipped, and stuffed. I'm no player, but that night I was on fire.

Our game was interrupted by a car winding its way up the gravel, kicking a cloud of dust behind it. Behind the wheel was a broad-shouldered man. *Was it?* No. It couldn't be . . .

Scenery blurred as I watched the big, tall teddy bear of a guy stroll across the lawn toward the party. He was the 3-D match of my four-year dreams.

Evan. I breathed. *He's alive!*

For a moment the world went quiet. All I could hear was the slow, steady beat of my own heart. *Dun-dun. Dun-dun. Dun-dun.*

"Jen?" I heard someone say my name. "Jen!"

Everything whizzed back into action just in time for me to see the volleyball screaming toward me. Unprepared, I used the first body part I could think of to return the serve. Channeling my inner Mia Hamm at the World Cup, my right foot connected with the ball, sending it sailing into the blue sky, over the net, above the opposing team, and over Evan's head before landing in a distant neighbor's yard.

Everyone stared at me in silence. Then, in a stroke of luck, the grill master yelled, "Time to eat!" The party zipped back to life as the game dispersed and everyone headed inside.

Evan was now just ten feet away, standing on the lawn, checking his phone. Adrenaline surged inside me as the trumpeting intro of Rocky Balboa's theme song pumped through my veins.

This was the moment I'd been training for. Straightening my shoulders, I jumped into the imaginary ring, stepping toward him.

I could hear the inner voices wildly chanting my name from the stands. Behind me the scarlet sunset cast a hazy, romantic glow over the mountainous backdrop, creating an angelic halo above my soft brunette curls. It was like God draped the gingham Instagram filter over the world, for such a time as this.

With each step toward him, my confidence grew. I knew baseball stats, golf lingo, how to move through a crowd. I could rumba and mambo, play kickball, catch fish. I had masqued and moisturized and pumped my pores full of lycopene and peptide-8. I could shoot guns, recite Proverbs, and build a campfire in three minutes flat.

My lips, glossed in Golden Prism, widened into a radiant and inviting smile as I stood before him. He looked up from his phone and our eyes met. I extended my French-lavender-scented hand toward his.

"Hi, Evan." I nailed my intro line. "I'm Lisa's sister, Jen."

We shook hands, yet by the time I blinked, his grip had already released mine. Never had I seen anyone turn his back so fast in my entire life. It was all I could do to hope there was something terrifying behind me, like a bloodthirsty vampire, and it was every man and woman for themselves.

But when I turned to look over my shoulder, there was nothing. Nothing but wide, Wild West skies. He had gotten my message, that much was clear. And without him using a single word, I had gotten his.

I stood by myself on that lawn, confused, annihilated, watching him walk away. Chest pounding, I looked down at my new first-date tank, jeans, and lightweight sweater. With nowhere to hide, I swallowed the lump in my throat, fighting back the sting in my eyes.

Taking a deep breath, I hung my head and made my way inside.

Gifts

Perhaps Evan felt guilty for blowing me off, or maybe he feared being struck by a punishing lightning bolt from God. Either way, he and I went on to have a few moments of forced conversation at dinner.

After that, I'm not sure where he went because I planted myself next to a sweet girl with Midwest roots and made small talk about consoling topics like knitting, *Anne of Green Gables*, and homemade apple pie.

When it came time for gifts later that night, I set my polka-dotted box with the bright red bow on Lisa's lap. "Happy thirtieth, sister."

There was a slight quiver to my voice and I blushed, hoping no one could tell I was one breath away from completely falling apart. Returning to my seat, I didn't look around the room to see where Evan was. I didn't care to know.

Tearing off the paper, Lisa lit up like a disco ball. "YESSSS!!!" Hopping to her feet, she pulled the freshly washed, worn-in gray hoodie over her head, then slid both arms into the sleeves. They hung three inches off each hand.

"How do I look?" She spun for the room, arms flapping in the breeze.

"Let's just say . . . I can't believe it took you thirty years to look this good, Lis." I winked. Everyone laughed as she struck a pose. On the outside, I laughed too. But deep down, all I wanted to do was cry.

Distractions

"Chai lattes are on me!" Lisa chirped, spinning toward the counter of her favorite local coffee shop wearing my old gray hoodie for the second day in a row. On her head was the other gift I'd given her: a pair of oversized glittery sunglasses, one plastic lens shaped liked a three, the other shaped like a zero.

It was Wednesday morning, and our cars were packed outside. We were meeting for one hour to create The Final Showdown, September's monthly theme, before hitting the road for home.

Lisa had just come from a breakfast date down the street. We had been in town for only a few days, but that hadn't stopped her friends from setting her up with some cowboy. I, of course, was not on a date. Instead, I had waited for her, checking my emails at the coffee shop alone.

We hadn't talked much about Evangate. Lisa had texted him and a couple other friends after her birthday party, inviting them out with us that night, though she did not tell me this until we departed for the restaurant.

Though I dreaded the thought of seeing him, I wasn't mad at her. I knew it was Lisa's way of shooting one more arrow from Cupid's bow. Her way of trying to make things right.

Evan did stop by, and conversation was exactly as painful as you would expect, given how our first introduction went. I figured he showed up either because he didn't realize he'd behaved poorly or because he knew it all too well. It no longer mattered; that four-year dream had crumbled to the ground.

While Lisa was the kind of person who listens, she wasn't really the type of person to press. Without saying a word, we both knew she was there if I wanted to talk. Instead, after her party, I quietly packed up my tears, swear jar, and wounds, saving them for my fifteen-hour drive back to Denver, like a cooler filled with snacks.

"Ta-da!" Lisa interrupted my thoughts, setting thick mugs of spicy chai in front of our chairs. Wrapping my hands around its sides, I pulled it close, thankful for a distraction from the funeral happening inside my heart.

Pulling out the pink notebook from my backpack, I flipped through past months' notes and journal entries and points. There were just three blank pages left.

"All right," I said, taking the pen from behind my ear. "Let's get this party started." It was refreshing to be seated face-to-face with my challenger, instead of communicating via the airwaves between the Colorado Rockies and the Idaho plains.

Smoothing a crisp, clean page with the palm of my hand, I wrote the word *strengths* across the top in bold letters, then drew a line down the middle, creating two columns. One for me, the other for Lisa. I labeled a second piece of paper *opportunities,* then divided it like the first.

Until now, our point system was designed like a big, cozy muumuu: one-size-fits-most. Meeting men, dating more, working out, seeking mentors, plus all our monthly themes were disciplines that would benefit most any single person.

But now, in one final thirty-day blitz, we were cinching up our muumuus, measuring each of our individual strengths and opportunities in dating. Lisa and I were different people. We had different gifts and unique dating hurdles to overcome. So, in September, there would be two different point systems. One tailored to help me and another to help her.

We started by identifying our strengths, pouring affirmations into one another's columns. What were each of us great at? How had we seen the other person grow? What qualities about our competitor really impressed us? Celebrating each other seemed like the right place to start.

"You're like a man whisperer, Lis." My eyes were wide with awe as I took a sip of chai. "It's been amazing to see your confidence with the Meet Men challenge. You're fearless when it comes to walking up to new guys and giving them your info."

I paused, jotting down key words in her "Strengths" column: "Man whisperer. Confident. Meet Men challenge. Fearless. Lighthearted."

"Well, I can't believe how many dates you've pushed yourself to go on, Jen." It was Lisa's turn to be blown away. "Considering the fact that you didn't really start earning points until the end of April, you've gone on nearly forty dates in four months! That's more than double what I've done."

I nodded, amazed at the number. She continued, noting the ways I kept showing up, even when it was hard. Pulling the notebook toward her, she added key words into my column: "Dating ninja. Openhearted. Committed. Vulnerable. Courageous."

We looked at monthly themes as well, jotting down that Lisa was a natural during Conversation Starters and Learning to Speak Man. Then we noted how hard I worked during our Venues Challenge and shined during A Beautiful Way.

Next, we moved onto areas of opportunity, those we saw either in each other or in ourselves.

Lisa and I agreed my biggest areas of opportunity were using Conversation Starters and giving guys my info with the Meet Men challenge. I felt intimidated by both, so during September those were the two main ways I could earn points.

Going on dates and the Venues Challenge were Lisa's biggest areas of opportunity. She admitted that she'd been a bit apathetic in those categories due to her geographic location. And so, during September those were the two core ways she could earn points.

We also discussed how working out and Couples Therapy had helped us become better singles and, thus, better daters. To our surprise and joy, both of those bonus challenges had increased our energy, confidence, and happy hormones. They both improved our moods when the dating challenge felt hard. And so, we would continue earning points for both during September as well.

I titled our last notebook page "The Final Showdown," then outlined our new point structure. Instead of being one-size-fits-most, it was tightened up, customized, tailored to challenge us in unique and individual ways.

The Final Showdown

Jen	Lisa
• Meet Men – 50 points/each • Couples Therapy – 25 points/each • Conversation Starters – 10 points/each • Working out – 10 points/each	• First Dates – 50 points/each • Couples Therapy – 25 points/each • Venues Challenge – 10 points/each • Working out – 10 points/each

"Well, that's a wrap." I said, shutting the notebook. "In just a few short weeks, one of us will be crowned the Dating Champion of the World."

Lisa slid her new oversized glittery sunglasses onto her face. "And I'm in the lead!" She stood with a dorky smile, grabbing our empty mugs and making her way to the barista.

It felt good to laugh, something I hadn't done since Evan's rejection. I stood, too, and packed my things: the notebook, my bruised heart, and a to-go coffee for the drive back home. Walking outside into the crisp September air, Lisa and I hugged good-bye.

The cool mountain breeze blew my hair across my face as I fumbled for the keys to my car. "Oh, hey, Lis?" I called out after her.

"Yeah, Jen?" She looked back, pulling the glitzy "3-0" birthday shades off her face.

"I meant to ask you this inside. We've come this far. Just twenty-seven days left. What exactly are you hoping to get out of this crazy dating challenge?"

She stood thoughtfully for a moment, then shrugged, her long sleeves hanging at her sides. "I already got what I wanted, Jen. I got to spend time with you."

Chapter 17 | Crossroads

"Oh yes, the past can hurt. But the way I see it,
you can either run from it or learn from it."

~ *Rafiki,* The Lion King

Pulling onto the highway, I stared through my bug-spattered windshield at my bleak fifteen-hour view. My cruise control and radio were as broken as my ego, leaving only the hum of my engine to break the silence.

Minutes ticked by, and soon the movie reel began to play . . .

I'm walking across the lawn toward Evan, the hazy sunset hitting my hair just right. My conversation skills are sharp, and I've got interesting things to say. I'm the most polished, 2.0 version of me I've ever been. Smiling warmly, lips freshly glossed, I extend my hand toward his. And then . . .

Clouds roll in. Thunder rumbles. My face morphs, sprouting a unibrow, a third eye, and an open-mouthed, Napoleon-Dynamite stare. Like an annoying GIF you're so over but addicted to in the same breath, the scene where Evan turned his back on my handshake played on repeat.

On repeat.

On repeat.

Tumbleweed blew across the shadowed highway as I continued to replay every move. My chest tightened, and for the first time since he'd turned and walked away, I gave space for my tears to fall.

I drove that way for a long time. Right foot steady on the pedal. Mile markers flying by. Endless, lifeless, barren plains. No music. No cell service. No cruise control. Just the loud hum of my engine—and space to say good-bye to that four-year dream.

Cupped in my hands, held close to my heart, there had been the hope of meeting someone wonderful, someone trustworthy, someone great. But instead, my hope had collided with my deepest fear, like a colossal ocean wave smashing a ship deck, splintering boards and shredding sails. Releasing my handshake, he turned his back and walked away, sending one crushing swell, then the next.

To be honest with you, I wanted to blame Evan for the state of my heart. It would have been easy to fill a swear jar or maybe even two. Easy to shake my fist at the sky while shouting, "I bet he likes strawberry ice cream!"

But the longer I watched the replay like a coach reviewing a game, I knew Evan only held as much power as I was willing to give him.

Decisions

Staring at the open road, my mind shot through memories of the woman I was before the stories of our dating challenge began. Slayed on my couch, I sported a marshmallow mocha mustache and my "It Took Me 30 Years to Look This Good" hoodie. I lacked energy, was full of excuses. I was chained by tens of thousands of dollars in debt, in a career without movement. There was my smashed-up car and my Goji Berry red lips, guilty as charged. A jam-packed Netflix queue. And me: buried and stuck, feeling behind in every possible way.

Before our sisters' camping trip, I washed then wrapped in polka-dotted paper not just a gray sweatshirt but a symbol. Though I had no idea how things would go with Evan, I knew no matter what happened, it was time to say good-bye to that girl, that woman. The one lying on her couch each Friday night, watching rom-coms alone, wishing, wanting, waiting, hoping . . .

For almost one year, I had been making room. Making room for change, for bravery, for love. And now I saw clearly my greatest crossroad of all.

Sure, I could let Evan define my value, giving in to those voices telling me it would be safer to go back to the way things used to be. A time when I controlled my risk, never putting myself out there, a life without hurt or rejection or pain.

Or . . . I could continue doing things that scared me. I could show up to the gym wearing matching socks and step up to a new guy and ask for his help, risking my life, or at least risking my ego. I could email five new men and celebrate the courage, not the outcome.

I could get up early and go for a walk and pick up extra side gigs in order to blast through my chains and become debt free. I could gently work my way into a circle of people at a Meetup group and say something clever, like "Hi, I'm Jen." I could be proud when all those small acts of bravery continue to change me, one small step at a time.

I could forgive myself for letting a four-year fantasy sweep my heart away. And then I could look in the mirror and believe for myself and about myself: I *am* enough. Not too much. And I could be free.

Now only one decision remained: which *me* would I choose to be?

Clearly

Dusk had settled over Wyoming, and my headlights pierced the darkness. My phone screen lit up as a tower came into view. After hours of silent processing, I finally had service.

Keeping my eyes on the road, I instructed Siri to call Emily.

"Hey, Jen!" she picked up.

"Hey, Em," I responded. My tension softened at the sound of her care. "Have a few minutes to chat?"

"Sure do," she replied. "You okay?"

"I, um, I need to process with someone."

For the next hour, Emily let me talk and I let myself need. I talked about my year of transformation, the dating challenges, and the smoke-and-mirrors relationship I'd given way too much of my heart and head space to.

She gave me space to feel. She offered gentle, encouraging words to take with me. And by the end of it all, I felt like her arm was linked into mine. I was wiser, smarter, and stronger with Em by my side.

Before saying good-bye, she stopped me.

"Jen." She paused.

"Yeah, Em?"

"Thanks for needing me."

Her tender words went straight to my core. I *did* need her. More than she would ever know. In fact, if it hadn't been for Emily's unconditional admiration, my life would still be the same.

"I love you, Em."

"Love you too."

After hanging up, I took a deep breath. Throughout my trip, there had been one person from back home on my mind. He was a quarter inch taller than I was and had a booming voice and a heart of gold. Peace settled over me as I made my next call.

"Hey Siri, call Will."

"Calling Will," she responded.

My heart skipped a beat at the sound of his voice. "Hey, Jen!" The enthusiasm with which he said my name felt like being greeted by the wagging tail of one's most faithful companion. "How was your camping trip?"

I told him all the very best parts: making air-guitar campsite music videos with my sisters to pass the time, mountaintop views that took my breath away, and crackling fires each cool night under the stars.

Pausing, I waited for him to ask about Lisa. In all my dreaming and scheming to set them up, I imagined my excessive seed-planting was making him curious about her. But he didn't ask about Lisa. He asked about me.

"So, what are you doing this Friday night? We're having a dinner party for my good friend's birthday." He paused. "I'd love if you joined me."

The amount of genuine care in his voice shot like Cupid's arrow straight through my heart. For the last few months, the distraction of Glacier stood like a six-hundred-pound grizzly in front of me.

I had been so focused on a fabricated dream guy a thousand miles away that I hadn't allowed myself to see the awesome man in front of me the whole time. But things were clearer now, like the day in third grade I slipped on my first pair of tortoise-shell glasses the size of my face. I could finally see the writing on the wall.

"I'd love to, Will," I said. Just then, my beams hit the rugged "Welcome to Colorful Colorado" sign.

I was almost home.

Chapter 18 | The Final Showdown

"May the force be with you."

~ *Yoda,* Star Wars: A New Hope

Will and I stood side by side chopping romaine in his friends' open kitchen. Big band music mixed with laughter filtered in from the living room as all fourteen dinner guests arrived.

"You must be Jen." A girl with green eyes and a freckled nose walked over, gently touching my arm. "I'm Jess. And this is my husband, Ben." She gestured to the gentleman walking over with two lemonades in his hands.

Ben gave Jess a drink, then shook my hand. "We've heard so many great things about you, Jen!" Will's face flushed.

The group gathered in the kitchen to bless the meal. Everyone took a hand as we bowed our heads. The warmth of Will's palm in my left and Jess's in my right instantly made me feel at home.

For the rest of the evening we sat on the patio sharing a meal under the stars. Conversation breezed between laughter and depth; it was easy to see that his people were my kind of people too.

Will was warm and welcoming that night, an encourager and leader around his friends. His worn Henley didn't point toward his need for a wardrobe update, like I'd maybe thought before. Instead, I was beginning to see the real him. A guy who was good with his money, kind, responsible, generous to those in need.

I wasn't sure what the future held, but I knew one thing: there were still good guys left in the world. And the more I'd focused on becoming the woman I was meant to be, one of those great guys had slowly and magically appeared.

What's Your Strategy?

"So, let me get this straight," I said to Lisa during our mid-September scoreboard update. My elbow was propped on the desk, chin resting in my hand.

"A tall, dark, and handsome male model from Brazil with a thick, dreamy Spanish accent asked you out."

"Yes," she replied.

"So, you took him on a romantic date to an Opera House . . ."

"That's right."

"Where the featured screening was a movie about mysterious radioactive ooze that mutated four sewer turtles into talking, upright-walking, crime-fighting ninjas."

"Yes, Jen. I took the cultured Brazilian hunk to see *Teenage Mutant Ninja Turtles*."

"Hmmm." I stared at her in unbroken silence. Dropping my hand, I nodded in approval. "I like the way you date, Lis."

The Final Showdown was testing my courage and her grit. I had resurrected the small, blue-bordered Conversation Starters checklist from April, and it stayed glued to the palm of my left hand at all times.

Each night after work, I'd stop by Target or Home Depot for nothing more than points. Pushing past seasonal décor, I'd browse a few aisles, practicing lines on any single guy I could find.

Some conversations resulted in 50 points while others simply gave me a chance to pump out a few bravery bicep curls. Day after day, week after week, I felt myself moving from Cowardly-Lion status to There's-a-New-Sheriff-in-Town.

"I underestimated you, Lis," I said after tallying our points for that week. In addition to three workouts and four Couples Therapy interviews, she zipped around the state going to several venues, plus had five dates in one week.

We stared at one another through the screen. I imagined we were standing on a dusty street in the old Wild West, coolly confronting each other in a deadly game of quick draw. There were two of us but only one crown.

"I'm planning to win, you know," Lisa said casually, plucking off a juicy red grape and popping it into her mouth. "I've been asking all my friends to help me get dates. One of them is hosting a dinner party to set me up." She paused for dramatic effect. "It's set for two days before our challenge ends."

I didn't like the glimmer in her eyes. "What about you, Jen?" she added. "What's your strategy?"

"My strategy?" I froze, imagining Lisa at her upcoming dinner party, surrounded by the entire male cast of last season's *Bachelorette*, all feeding her the juicy red grapes she now had in her hand. *How did I ever think I could compete against Lisa?*

"My strategy?" I said, arching my brow with faux confidence. "No excuses."

Change

The next morning, I jumped out of bed, threw on a pot of coffee, hopped in the shower, lathered, shampooed, shaved, and conditioned all in six minutes flat. Sure, I had ninety-nine problems, but my energy was no longer one of them.

Wrapping my hair in a towel, I pulled my work clothes off their hangers. I had a full day ahead of me: teaching facial massage techniques at a spa, conducting Couples Therapy after work, then swinging by the gym for a quick date with the elliptical.

Slipping each leg into my black dress slacks, I couldn't help but notice that even after buttoning them, they slipped right off. Throwing them on the floor, I grabbed another pair. Same story, different pants.

I stepped from the hardwood onto the cool plastic base of my scale. When the three red numbers appeared, my jaw hit the floor.

That week was the one-year anniversary of being sentenced to driving probation. I had steadily lost exactly one pound per week since last fall. No pills, no cutting carbs, no shakes, no crash dieting. Just good old-fashioned showing up, one sluggish workout, one balanced meal at a time.

A year ago, one mile had been tough and Netflix with takeout was my go-to way to unwind. That had evolved over time. Now, brisk five-mile walks that broke into an occasional light jog was my favorite way to decompress after a long day.

Standing on the scale, I faced a new problem: I was all out of pants. Not that I was complaining.

Chains Falling

A few days later, I jolted from my sleep. Flying into a sitting position and straight as a board, I yanked off my eye mask and sent it flying across the room.

Fumbling for my phone on the nightstand, I took a deep breath, then punched in my bank information. Affirmative: it was pay day.

My fingers typed as fast as they could move as a series of questions appeared.

"Please select the recipient of your online payment." SALLIE MAE STUDENT LOANS

"What amount would you like to send?" $487.16

"Does this information look correct?" YES

"Are you sure you want to proceed?" YES! I responded, wringing my phone.

A colorful wheel appeared on the screen, spinning, spinning, spinning, and then, it disappeared. In its place were four words: "Your payment is complete."

I stared at my phone in the early morning silence. Heart racing, blood pumping, heart cheering, chains dropping, life changing.

After graduating college at the end of my twenties, I carried over $50,000 in debt. Even after four years of hard work and paying off $27,000 ahead of schedule, I found myself bone tired of scrimping and scraping by.

And so, I began the hardest, most financially sacrificial year of my life.

Over twelve months, and against all odds, I'd paid off the remaining $23,222.78. Lifting my chin to the sky, I felt my chains crash to the ground, one right after another. Throwing my arms into a V, a power pose that had never felt quite right until now, I smiled and whispered three words.

"I'm debt free."

One Week Remaining

Lisa and I shot into our final week of the competition like two champion racehorses on their final lap. The $100 spa gift card was in mouthwatering view. And the winning title, Dating Champion of the World, was so close we could feel the silk sash across our bodies, the weight of the crown on our heads.

Half cheerleader, half rogue cowgirl, Lisa and I each had a pom-pom in one hand and a pistol in the other. During that last week, from the moment we woke to the second our heads hit our pillows each night, we text bombed as part of our ongoing war. Then we stepped back, each of us silently cheering the other sister on.

"Just met Brandon, new single guy at Starbucks. Boom." I hit the microphone emoji to signal a mic drop, then finished with "50 points by 8:00 a.m. . . . and it's only Monday!"

Within minutes, Lisa responded, "Double header today. Lunch with Andy at one. Dinner with Patrick at six. 100 points."

I saw the little dot-dot-dot on the screen, signaling she was typing another message. A microphone emoji appeared, followed by another dot-dot-dot. "She wouldn't dare." My eyes narrowed as I chugged espresso from my carafe. Then a second microphone appeared.

"Two mic drops." I shook my head; my left eye twitched. "She dared."

Left Foot. Right Foot.

Walking up to the gym on September 29, I paused in front of the big faithful tree that had kept me company through every season that year. As if giving me a cheerful hello, sunrays broke through its radiant fall leaves, warming my skin in the cool morning air.

There were forty hours left on the clock, and Lisa was ahead by 10 points. Her dinner party was that night, which included a blind date, thanks to begging friends to set her up with any eligible guys they knew. That meant that by tonight I'd need 60 points to tie and even more to take the lead. Plus, who knew what else Lisa had tucked up her sleeve?

Music kicked on in the cycling studio just past the elliptical machines, reminding me why I was there. Today I was going to try spin class.

It had been a couple of years since my last spin class, so I selected a bike in the shadows of an empty back row. Within minutes a single gentleman walked in and grabbed the bike to my right. The studio door reopened, and another bachelor took the one on my left. No longer hidden, I took a swig from my water bottle and tried to act natural, waiting for class to begin.

Following the instructor's lead, we started to move. With each push of the pedal, panoramic mountaintop views flashed before my eyes. Back in Glacier and on top of the world, I rolled my tires to the edge of the pavement.

Left foot. Right foot. Left foot. Right foot.

Four pedal strokes were all it took to gain the momentum I needed. *No excuses*, I breathed, reaching for the knob to increase my resistance. Lifting off my seat, we began our first climb.

"Hey," I said, breathless, turning first to my left, then my right. "I'm Jen!"

One nodded. "I'm Jake."

"Jeremy," the other said.

"Crank that dial, folks!" the instructor yelled out. Conversation faded into fast and focused drills.

Forty minutes later, the cooldown began. My legs, now Jell-O, slowed to the beat. Dripping with sweat, high on endorphins, and face beet red, I restarted the conversation. By the time I left class, both guys had my info. And I had 110 points.

Standing on the sidewalk, I held my hand against the midmorning sun. There in front of me, explosions of fire-engine-red leaves mingled with scarlet, blush, and lime green.

Struck by its beauty and loved by its presence, I watched in awe as a gentle breeze tickled that old faithful tree. Instantly each leaf came alive, a rainbow of colors, bursting into thunderous applause.

Dropping my hand, I stood and let its shadows dance across my face. My internal world was crystal clear. I was fearless. I was brave. I was enough.

I was free.

I Am

Settling into the soft white piles of down blankets layering my bed, I sighed. It was October. Hugging a pillow to my chest, I rolled onto my side and lay still.

The wildest 183 days of my life were finally over.

Making my way into the kitchen, I brewed a pot of coffee and grabbed a mug. In just a few hours, Lisa and I would log in to Zoom for the final scoreboard update. Both of us had finished strong; I had no idea who was getting the crown.

I sat down at the kitchen table and flipped open my Bible. My bookmark guided me to the place I last left off. Today's reading: Hosea, chapter 14.

As I read the ancient words, I couldn't believe what it said. *Am I reading this right?* It felt too personal, too relevant, too real. I leaned in, hovered over the page, racing through the passage a second time. Then a third.

With finger pressed onto the last paragraph of the thin page, tears stung my eyes as I read God's timely and closing claim: "I am that glorious tree, the source of your fruit. If you are wise, you will know and understand what I mean" (Hosea 14:8–9).

Underneath the passage, a simple footnote read "This is the only place in the Old Testament where the Lord is compared to a tree."

Closing my eyes, memories flooded through me. Instantly, I was transported to that first day back at my gym, seeing the sun filter in through those tree branches, highlighting an elliptical in the front row. Climbing on, sluggish and stuck, I stared at leaves being plucked and pulled from its branches, wondering if my life would ever change.

Through winter, spring, summer, and fall, I always chose the same spot at the gym, enjoying the beauty, stability, and camaraderie of that tall stoic tree. Every few months, I would snap a photo of it. Each seasonal transfiguration spoke to me, without using a single word.

Tears fell from my eyes, hitting the thin pages of my Bible as I read the verse again.

Sometimes God was quiet, but he had always been there—guiding, leading, whispering, calling. And little had I known, the transformation I always prayed for would come after turning to him inwardly with my heart, then outwardly with my life.

Chapter 19 | The Wedding

"You've always had the power, my dear. You just had to learn it for yourself."

~ Glinda the Good Witch, The Wizard of Oz

One year, seven months, and eight days later . . .

It was the weather every bride dreams of having on her wedding day. Uncharacteristically warm for a May afternoon in Minnesota, blue skies climbed as far as the eye could see.

April spring rains had done what they do best, giving life to the sharp green lawns and budding trees surrounding the 125-year-old church building where my family attended when I was growing up. It was absolute perfection.

My nephew stood just over three feet tall. His brow furrowed into a terribly adorable don't-look-at-me grumpy face and a wooden sign bearing the phrase "Here Comes the Bride" hung loosely around his bow-tied neck. His older sister twirled around him in all her flower girl glory, radiating a sparkling joy as if the day was her very own.

My brother and the other groomsmen stood tall, rugged, handsome, with hands in pockets, quietly small-talking in the back of the old church foyer. My dad joined them, his kind blue eyes dancing against his tanned skin and silver hair. Today was the day he would give the first of his three daughters away in marriage.

The church sanctuary filled, bursting with beloved family and close friends while the clock on the foyer wall revealed we were just moments away from opening the old double doors that divided the bridal party from the guests. The wedding was about to begin.

Emily, Lisa, our sister-in-law, Ashley, and I slipped our arms around one another's waists, stealing a quiet moment of whispered prayers and encouragement for the sacred vows that were about to take place. Then we drew one another in for one tight final prewedding sister hug.

It was time.

Stepping through the doorway and into the sanctuary, I was met with row after row of lifelong relationships, a beautiful sea of familiar faces. My fingertips clasped the silk ribbon, wrapped firmly around stems of citrus ranunculus, blushing roses, and soft white hydrangeas. Drifting down the aisle, my eyes locked with the groom.

Then, with a deep breath, I lifted the hem of my floor-length navy chiffon dress and stepped past him, making my way to the top of the stairs. I stood there, breath held, taking it all in, as rays of afternoon sun danced through the panes of old stained-glass windows high above our heads.

Moments later, the pianist's fingertips lingered on her last notes, coming to a brief pause before beginning the bride's processional. Heads turned once again to the back of the sanctuary as the wooden double doors reopened. Both mothers stood and the congregation followed as Lisa, dressed in white, crossed the threshold, arm in arm with our dad.

Joy spread across my face as I watched her—my sister, my competitor, my cofounder, my friend—in all her beauty, walk toward her groom. Each step she took down the rich burgundy carpet brought to life so much fulfillment for all the hard work, all the dreaming, and all the becoming that had been done during those unforgettable six months.

Neither of us could have ever predicted that a Friday night phone call and one half-joking dare could change our lives in so many ways. Our story was bigger than just finding love. We had found ourselves.

In the last forty hours of our competition, Lisa went to that dinner party her friend had arranged in their small Idaho town. The whole goal of the party was to help Lisa get more points. On the guest list, there was one single guy she'd never met: Andrew, a tall, introspective musician with deep Midwest roots.

Before the setup, her friend commented that she didn't know Lisa's type. In response, Lisa offered a casual shrug. "It's not like I'm going to marry the guy!" And yet, one year, seven months, and eight days later, there we were. He was a teacher, an artist, a techie, a wordsmith, with a deep and thoughtful soul.

They were better together—like Mario and Luigi, hot fudge and vanilla, coffee and scones.

Standing on the burgundy carpet, I watched our dad kiss Lisa's cheek, then give her away. The groom's eyes were filled with joy as he looked down at his beautiful bride.

In that moment I knew who the real winner of our dating challenge was . . .

Congratulations, Andrew.

Dating Champion of the World

All right, so which sister actually won the dating competition? Which one of us wears the silky sash and will never let the other live it down?

It's like I told Lisa at the beginning of this book. When it comes to fake crowns and fictitious titles, I stop at nothing. After six months and with a mere 10-point lead, I, Jen Carlson, was crowned the Dating Champion of the World.

(Insert me, sitting in the back of a red-hot convertible, flashing my pearly whites and waving like Miss America while Lisa tosses sparkly confetti above my head.)

Before the dating challenge, I reserved "showing up" for someday. Someday when I'm in shape, I'll show up. Someday when I've got more time and energy, with less on my plate, that's when I can start showing up. Someday when I'm confident, or when a guy shows interest, or right after a total makeover—that's when I'll start showing up. But for one entire year, I decided to change that, and my life will never be the same.

Transformed

In the months following our competition, I sent out my first Christmas card in years; a picture of me wearing that new outfit in Montana, surrounded by farm goats Lisa and I had found off an old country road. "Merry Christmas!" It read. "Love, Jen and the kids."

That same season, my company called with big news. Not only did they offer me that promotion I dreamed of, they also wanted to double the increase I originally asked for. That month, I finished reading the Bible from front to back.

Soon after, I bought my first home in Denver, a two-bedroom condo with vaulted ceilings, a cozy loft, and a charming stone fireplace. I increased my tithing too. After that, I saved up and paid cash for a new (used) car.

To this day I am beyond grateful I painfully hustled my debt before getting that raise. Now I know it's not money that frees us. It's sacrifice, discipline, and the good old-fashioned power of blood, sweat, and tears.

Changing my financial future gave me the flexibility and freedom to become licensed in foster care. When I did a deep dive on that Bible passage in Hosea, I discovered when we turn wholeheartedly to God, he gives us roots like a mighty tree too. Connection with him enables our branches to spread. Our ability to provide shade and respite enlarges. And the joy is all mine; it brings me so much happiness loving on teens in this new way.

As for Will, he and I dated for some time, though we eventually chose to part ways. I look back on that relationship as fun, memorable, positive, and pure. If it weren't for the dating challenge, pushing me outside my list, I would never have given a great guy like Will a fighting chance. I'd still be stuck on the Evans of this world, those imaginary soul mates that exist only in our dreams.

And as for me, I'm single again, making room for new goals and, of course, for love. If there's one thing I learned from that year of transformation, it's never to let my present circumstances, my future fears, or my past disappointments hold me back from becoming the woman I was created to be.

So how does a dating competition story end when the girl hasn't found her guy? I guess that is what's different about this book; it doesn't have an ending. Just a new beginning filled with vision, hope, and the courage to try again.

Acknowledgments

Emily and Lisa: My inspirer and my competitor, my sisters, my friends. No one sees all the best and worst of me yet continues to love me as deeply and truly as you. You have read every first, third, seventh, and tenth draft with patience and the brutal, gut-punching honesty that only sisters can give. Thanks for linking arms with me on this journey, from cover to cover, for better or for worse, in sickness and in health, for as long as we each shall live.

Mom and Dad: You've always made sure your cheering and encouragement were louder than any other voice in this world. Thanks for planting seeds of faith, family, love, and a desire to serve the Lord in my life. Those seeds have become deep roots. So much of who I am today is because of you.

Brian and Ashley: What a gift to have you as my accountability squad during my debt-freedom journey. Sacrifices were easier knowing you guys were down in the trenches doing the hard work too. I love you both. Also, we're debt freeeee!

Andrew and Kelton: Andrew, thanks for the Sedaris book, the vintage typewriter, and for being the best thing to come out of this dating challenge. Kelton, your enthusiasm for life, intentional question-asking, and your partnership with Em are so admirable. Thank you both for encouraging me from your courts.

Karen Bouchard: I'm forever grateful for your early eyes on this project, helping me understand book development and the larger themes at work. Your enthusiasm was the magic fairy dust I needed to begin weaving these stories together.

Deb Hall: You are a copyediting ninja, a steady voice, a fellow writer-turned-friend. You've been the person I have counted on from first draft to publishing day, helping me create order from chaos. I'm so thankful for all the ways you've given me confidence in the craft.

Anne Horowitz: Your developmental editing became a turning point for this story. Without your direction, this book would be Swiss cheese, full of holes begging to be filled. Thank you for pushing me deeper into backstory. This book is a million times better because of you.

Illumify Media: Mike, Jen, Geoff, and Lisa—you talked me off ledges and kept me steadily moving toward each deadline. You are advice givers, pom-pom wavers, and deeply knowledgeable experts about the publishing world. Thanks for helping me cross the finish line!

Adly Elewa: When it came to the final cover design, you jumped in and saved the day. You are upbeat, lightning fast, a creative powerhouse. I trust you with my life. Great design work is everything, and you exceeded expectations.

Month 5 Couples Therapy interviewees: To Peggy and Aaron, Jay and Erin, Mom and Dad, Jen and Chris, Ashley and Bryan, Ann Marie and Jon, Erik and Alyssa, Dave and Kristialyn, Ryan and Lynsie, Brian and Ashley, Kim and Dave, Eric and Amanda, Curt and Barb, Rich and Chris, Matt and Amanda. You brought so much laughter, joy, vulnerability, encouragement, and fun to the final months of my challenge. I hit the jackpot with friends like you.

My incredible community: A special thank-you to my brunch babes, Bible study girls, Cambridge besties, WaFaRa intern fam, RRC Life Groups, FPU crew, Writers on the Rock group, extended family, work colleagues, and so many more. Apparently, it takes a village to keep a fragile new author going, and your enthusiasm has been the fuel in my tank, the caffeine drip in my veins, the hype man before a big game. I'm so blessed by you.

My beautiful foster daughters: You are warriors, true examples of never giving up. I love you girls, forever and always.

My endorsers: Life is so busy, but you made time to read and support this book during the holidays before publication. Your generosity of spirit, time, and words will never be forgotten.

The single guys in our dating competition: Thanks for the part you each played in these stories. Dating is hard work for all of us, so no matter your role, Lisa and I are better because of you. Go get 'em, tigers.

And to Jesus: My God, my Savior, my truest and closest friend. You are the author and perfector of my faith, the beginning and end of my story. Thank you for giving me purpose and joy in this life, no matter what my relationship status is. I love because you first loved me.

About the Author

Jen Carlson is a writer and skin care territory manager in Denver, Colorado (saving lives one wrinkle at a time).

Jen's desire is to use her single season to love God and serve others, then inspire others to do the same. Jen became a licensed foster parent for the Unaccompanied Refugee Minor (URM) program in 2020 and has since hosted four teens and one sweet baby girl.

In her free time, Jen lives for salted OREO ice cream, hot pink nail polish, and creating fun memories with family and friends. Connect with her here:

Website: www.JenCarlson.com
Instagram: @_JenCarlson
Facebook: www.Facebook.com/JenCarlsonWrites

CPSIA information can be obtained
at www.ICGtesting.com
Printed in the USA
BVHW031522170123
656441BV00005B/848

9 781959 099062